Citrus and Tropical Fruit Trees
A Monograph on Planting, Culture and Care

by R.M. Teague Nurseries

with an introduction by Roger Chambers

This work contains material that was originally published in 1921.

This publication was created and published for the public benefit, utilizing public funding and is within the Public Domain.

This edition is reprinted for educational purposes and in accordance with all applicable Federal Laws.

Introduction Copyright 2018 by Roger Chambers

Self Reliance Books

Get more historic titles on animal and stock breeding, gardening and old fashioned skills by visiting us at:

http://selfreliancebooks.blogspot.com/

Introduction

I am pleased to present yet another title on Gardening.

The work is in the Public Domain and is re-printed here in accordance with Federal Laws.

As with all reprinted books of this age that are intended to perfectly reproduce the original edition, considerable pains and effort had to be undertaken to correct fading and sometimes outright damage to existing proofs of this title. At times, this task is quite monumental, requiring an almost total "rebuilding" of some pages from digital proofs of multiple copies. Despite this, imperfections still sometimes exist in the final proof and may detract from the visual appearance of the text.

I hope you enjoy reading this book as much as I enjoyed making it available to readers again.

Roger Chambers

TEAGUE QUALITY BUD AND ROOT-SELECTED TREES.

IF there is one thing more than another that has tended to improve quality and bearing capacity of fruit trees, it is the selection of buds from record bearing trees in the propagation of citrus and tropical fruit plants. It is a subject that has been exhaustively studied by the Department of Agriculture and Experiment Stations, and of late years has found practical operation in the Fruit Growers Supply Company (a subsidiary corporation of the California Fruit Exchange), which, after years of close observation, has now sufficient record trees under its observation to form a reliable source of supply for selected citrus buds. In addition the Avocado Association is pursuing a similar line of action. Having for years been a consistent advocate of bud selection, and being keenly alive to the work already accomplished, we are growing all our citrus and Avocado trees only from certified selected buds obtaind from th Fruit Growers' Supply Company and the California Avocado Association, thereby insuring quality and quantity bearing trees to all our patrons.

But this of itself will hardly insure a profitable tree—the bud must have a good foundation; in other words the root stock and its proper development must be right. Here we put in force the elimination of the unfit. Every seedling tree that exhibits a weak or faulty root development is discarded; and when we discard fully forty per cent of our seedling trees every year because of faulty devlopment the reader will appreciate that we practice root selection as well as bud selection. These two basic principles rigidly enforced give us the nucleus or foundation for growing good trees. Then comes intelligent care—proper culture and training, so that the tree will be of good form and habit, capable of functioning along lines that will prove a pleasure and a source of profit to their owners. That our efforts have been appreciated by planters in general, is evidenced by the ever-increasing demand for Teague trees, not only in California, but throughout the citrus growing sections of the world: Old Mexico, South America, Cuba, Porto Rico, the Hawaiian Islands, the Philippines, Australia, South Africa, China, Japan and India.

Realizing the importance of some of the more desirable tropical fruits, we have lately added the growing of such varieties as give promise of having a commercial future in California horticulture, and their propagation is being carried out in the same painstaking manner that has made Teague citrus trees so well and favorably known.

We have endeavored to make the articles on care and culture explicit, so that those just engaging in this line of work will understand the procedure necessary to properly care for their trees. As stated elsewhere, the varying conditions both as to climate and soil, make it impossible to lay down any hard and fast rule, and the planter must rely on his own judgment, in cases where these two conditions make cultural changes necessary.

CITRUS AND SUB-TROPICAL FRUITS

THEIR CULTURE, CARE AND MARKETING

IN presenting this treatise on Citrus and Sub-Tropical fruits, it is our aim to give those interested in the culture of these fruits, such information and advice as our experience and observation, covering a great many years of active work along these lines, will warrant.

While space in a book of this kind necessitates being brief, we shall endeavor to touch on the essential points necessary to give the novice an insight into the habits, requirements, culture and care of those varieties we enumerate to enable him to at least start right in laying the foundation for a successful commercial orchard, or in growing the few trees necessary to supply the home with those fruits peculiar to our California climate.

It is with pardonable pride that we point to the many acres of profitable citrus orchards planted to Teague trees during the past thirty-three years, and we want to here thank our many friends and patrons, whose continued trade throughout all these years has not only enabled us to keep increasing our business, but has spurred us on to increased efforts in the production of better and more prolific stock. Starting in business we adopted the slogan, "When better trees are grown, Teague will grow them," and to that end we have and shall continue to put forth every effort to grow the best trees that experience and money can produce.

To within the last year we have devoted our entire time and attention to the growing of citrus fruit trees, but with the advent of some of the more promising sub-tropical fruits into the commercial fruit-growing industry of California, and realizing that there was a wide field for the propagation of these fruits if handled along the same lines that have proven so successful with us in citrus propagation, we decided to take up the growing of such varieties as in our judgment give promise of possessing commercial importance.

Knowing that for the successful propagation of the sub-tropical fruit trees, we must have land practically free from frost where the most tender plants can be grown in the open the year around, we have recently purchased a ninety-acre tract in La Habra Heights, northwest of the town of La Habra and just across the county line in Los Angeles County.

This tract of land is particularly well located for nursery purposes, being partially surrounded by low hills, which practically isolates it from the valley proper, removes the danger of damage from heavy winds, and being an entirely new sub-division reduces the danger of scale infestation to a minimum.

The elevation is sufficient to make it practically immune to frost damage to even the most tender plant, and the soil, a deep rich loam, washed in from the adjacent hills in ages past, insures a perfect and most vigorous root system which is really the foundation of all successful plant life. With this location we know we can produce and deliver to our customers the most perfect specimens of both citrus and sub-tropical trees.

While we shall in the future grow most of our stock in this new location, the many years of successful dealings and association with planters and dealers from the different citrus growing sections of the world, having been transacted from our San Dimas office, we deem it advisable to maintain our headquarters here, where we are perfectly equipped to handle and pack stock in the best possible condition for local or long distance shipment and where we are always glad to meet those interested in horticulture, show our stock and explain our methods of growing and selling trees.

A Fruit Growers Supply Company Washington Navel performance record tree

CITRUS FRUITS

It seems unnecessary to go into detail regarding the early introduction of citrus fruits in California; however, for the purpose of enlightening those not familiar with early events in the citrus history of the state, it will probably not be out of place to recite some of the more important occurrences connected with the industry that have added so much to California's horticultural wealth.

It is said that California owes the introduction of horticulture to the Mission Fathers who, first of all, planted fruit-bearing trees on the Pacific Coast.

Coming north from Lower California in 1769, they established their first Mission at San Diego and worked northward, locating Missions wherever conditions warranted. In all they established twenty-one Missions, and it is said that at all but three of these gardens and orchards were planted. These plantings ranged from just a few trees to several hundred and consisted chiefly of oranges, figs, grapes and olives.

It is interesting to note that all of these fruits are now important industries in California horticulture, although a hundred years elapsed after they were first introduced before they attained commercial importance.

It is said that the most extensive orange orchard of early planting was at the San Gabriel Mission, in this county, planted by "Father" Thomas Sanchez in the year 1804. Other small plantings were made in and around Los Angeles, the most notable of which was planted by William Wolfskill in what is now the heart of Los Angeles city, in the year 1841, and consisted of two acres. This acreage was added to from time to time, but as late as 1862 it is recorded that there were but 25,000 orange trees in the entire state, and fully half of these were in the Wolfskill orchards. Other sections of the state were also credited with some of the early plantings, all of which were grown from seed. These sections ranged from San Diego on the south to as far north as Shasta County.

A record bearing Valencia Late orange tree: a source of our selected bud supply.

It was not, however, until about 1870 that extensive acreages began to be planted at Riverside and elsewhere, when citrus culture gave evidence of becoming an important commercial enterprise.

The real foundation for California supremacy in citrus culture was laid by the introduction of the two historical Washington Navel orange trees, from which sprang the vast acreage of Navel orchards that now grace the landscape of California.

This variety was introduced into the United States by the Department of Agriculture in 1870 and propagated in the orange house at Washington, D. C. Two of these trees were sent to Mrs. L. C. Tibbets, of Riverside, in 1873. These two trees are now the most celebrated fruit trees in Riverside and are guarded with the most tender care by its citizens. In 1913 one was transplanted to the grounds of the Mission Inn by the late Colonel Roosevelt during one of his visits to Southern California, the other still stands at the head of Magnolia avenue, where it enjoys the distinction of an enclosure with a tablet telling of its accomplishments.

While the Washingon Navel played a most important part in California citrus culture, it remained for the Valencia Late to complete the fame of California as an all-the-year shipper of citrus fruits. Ripening just as the shipment of Navels is about over, its fine keeping qualities enables us to continue shipments over a period of four or five months, or until the first of the new Navel crop is ready for market.

Thus we are able to give the consumer fresh oranges every month in the year. These two varieties are the only ones grown on an extensive scale.

The Ruby Blood, Paper Rind St. Michael, Mediterranean Sweet, Joppa, and some of the Mandarin types are grown to a limited extent commercially, while the Seedling orange of the early days is fast becoming a thing of the past, many of the older orchards having been either taken out or budded over to Navels or Valencies, and no Seedling orchards are being planted.

Lemon growing did not become an important factor in California horticulture until some years after the orange. While there were scattering trees here and there, and even some small orchards, it was not until the early nineties that the industry began to assume importance.

In referring to a report issued by the State Board of Agriculture in 1891, we find an article by G. W. Garcelon of Riverside, entitled "Fifteen Years with the Lemon," in which he describes his efforts to work out the lemon problem so that California lemons could successfully compete with the foreign importation.

Referring to the superiority of the foreign lemon at that time he says: "Years ago my attention was drawn toward the apparent truth that California could not produce a good lemon, for the San Francisco market quoted foreign lemons at $5.00 and $6.00 per box, domestic, at $1.00 and $2.00, and even less. These last were always overgrown Seedling lemons, which should have left the trees months

A Eureka lemon performance tree from which Fruit Growers Supply Company buds are cut

before. But they grew larger, made fewer to the box, and made—yes, made those who used them, profane over their efforts to extract any juice from them."

Mr. Garcelon's efforts were confined principally to working out methods for holding over the winter lemons so that they could be marketed in the summer, which, at that time, was the only season of the year lemons were used.

Thanks to the efforts of Mr. Garcelon and others, whose faith in California lemons prompted them to spend their time and money in studying out successful methods of growing and handling this fruit, we are now able to give the consumer a better lemon than the imported ones.

On account of lemons being more tender than

oranges they are not so generallly planted, but the planting on the higher and more protected lands of the five southern counties, viz., San Diego, Orange, Los Angeles, Ventura and Santa Barbara, has assumed quite extensive proportions. There has also been able to successfully compete with the Florida fruit in the Eastern markets. This is due to two reasons; first, sufficient care has not been exercised in selecting types of fruit particularly adapted to our soil and climatic conditions; and secondly, we have

A fine type of bud supply Marsh Seedless pomelo tree.

been considerable lemon planting in the protected sections along the east side of the San Joaquin Valley.

The present moneyed value of California's annual lemon crop is about $12,000,000.00, so it will be seen that lemon culture has become an important factor in our horticultural outputs.

Pomelos (Grapefruit) are not being planted as extensively as either oranges or lemons. While they do extremely well and are prolific bearers, we have not always insisted on trying to market our fruit before it is thoroughly mature, thus giving the consumer the impression that we cannot grow a good pomelo.

With the advent of bud selection and state laws prohibiting the shipment of immature fruit we hope to put a superior quality of pomelos on the market, and thus demonstrate that we can supply the consumer with fruit equal to the best. Pomelos will grow wherever oranges do well, but reach a higher state of perfection in the interior valleys, where the day and night temperature during the summer months is more nearly uniform.

Another feature favorable to pomelo culture is the fact that they, in common with oranges, are being more generally used throughout the entire year, thus increasing their consumption to a great extent. This is particularly favorable for California, as our pomelos are at their best during the summer months when the Florida fruit is off the market.

With the improvement in types, and by holding our fruit until it is mature, we can establish a reputation for quality that will not only increase the consumption in the United States, but may lead to a large export trade to foreign countries where pomelos are at present very little known.

It will be of interest to note the increase of citrus products in this state. Beginning with the year 1883, when there were shipped out of Southern California 150 carloads of oranges; in 1886 the output had increased to 1,000 carloads; in 1890-'91 there were shipped 3920 carloads, and in 1898-'99 a total of 15,006 carloads were sent out. Of this amount 1,500 cars were lemons

Ten years later, for the season 1908-'09, there were 6,196 cars of lemons and 31,895 cars of oranges, a total of 38,091 cars from Southern California and 2,501 cars of oranges and lemons from points north of the Tehachapi.

For 1920 the total production of oranges was 18,700,000 boxes, and of lemons 4,500,000 boxes; the combined value of which was $54,125,000.

The present annual income from California's citrus crop is something like $50,000,000.00, and the value of the orchards themselves is approximately $400,000,000.00.

GROWING TEAGUE QUALITY TREES

It will no doubt be of interest to those engaged in citrus culture to know how we grow our nursery trees. We feel that the buyer is entitled to know what care and attention has been bestowed upon the trees he is paying out good money for and on which he expects to spend more money and time in bringing them to a profitable bearing stage. For upon the proper methods of budding, growing and handling of the young trees in the nursery row, largely depends the success or failure of the planter to realize a profitable orchard (it being assumed that he is going to do his part in caring for the orchard), we are sure that every planter wants to feel assured that the nurseryman has left nothing undone that might affect the future growth and productiveness of his orchard. With that idea in view, we shall briefly describe the essentials in the production of Teague quality trees.

As far as possible we grow our own seedling stock and for this purpose select the best sour orange seed available. In order to insure hardy plants, we sow our seed in the open and allow it to come up and make its first season's growth under natural conditions. In transplanting the young seedlings to the nursery row, we select only those showing the most vigor and hardiness, the remainder being discarded. Every care is exercised in digging to secure all the fibrous roots possible and extreme precaution is used in protecting the same from the sun and air while moving them from the seed-bed to the nursery row. We plant all of our stock fifteen inches apart in the row and the rows four feet apart. This allows plenty of room for irrigating, cultivating and hoeing and insures a strong, vigorous tree. Only such pruning is done as is necessary to keep the trunk of the young tree free from sprouts and side branches up from the surface of the ground some 6 or 8 inches.

The seedlings are allowed to make two summer's growth in the nursery row before they are budded. This gives us a seedling with sufficient strength and vigor to force a good thrifty bud. In budding, we aim to get the bud from six to eight inches above the surface of the ground, which allows plenty of room so that with ordinary care in planting there is no danger of getting the bud set below the level of the soil—a condition that is almost sure to be fatal to all varieties of budded citrus trees, especially if planted on heavy land.

The budding is done in the fall and spring, October and November being the two falls months in which it is done and April and May the usual time for spring budding. The advantage of fall budding is that they heel in, but do not make any growth until spring, when they are ready to start with the first flow of sap and are usually a foot or more high before it is possible to begin the spring budding.

BUD SELECTION

One of the most important parts in the growing of good nursery stock, and one which we have always given very close attention, is the matter of selecting good buds and we point with pardonable pride to the many profitable orchards in different parts of California grown from trees of our own raising. Realizing that in order to produce trees yielding good crops of high grade fruit, it is necessary to select buds from the best and most prolific types of the varieties desired, we have always exercised every precaution to get only the best.

With the advent of what is known as pedigreed or selected buds, that is the selection of buds taken from trees having a record for quality and quantity productiveness, we have decided to use only this kind of buds. For the purpose of enabling the reader to realize the importance of this feature, we will give a brief history of the events leading up to the establishment of the bud selection department of the Fruit Growers' Supply Company.

Going back to the time when the orchard industry was in its infancy, when what few orchards there were consisted almost entirely of seedling orange trees, grown from seed selected at random from trees producing desirable types of fruit, little attention was paid to any particular selection of seed or plants and the grower who made any effort to select seed from any particular type of orange was considered to be wasting his time. Just so the fruit was edible was all that was considered necessary. About the time the importance of the Washington Navel orange became established, there was also introduced into the state a type of Navel orange known as the Australian Navel, a variety or type somewhat similar, but in every way inferior, to the Washington Navel, its chief objection being that the tree was a shy bearer. Both types were seedless, or nearly so, and the only method of reproduction was by budding.

The Washington Navel being so much superior to the old seedling varieties, the demand for trees stimulated the growing of citrus nursery stock, which up to that time had been mostly supplied by Florida nurserymen. Later many of the bearing seedling orchards were budded over to Navels, some of these seedling trees being 25 or 30 years of age. The demand for budwood taxed the young Navel orchards to the limit with the result that budwood was often taken from the Australian Navels, either through ignorance or indifference on the part of the person gathering buds. In this way the earlier orchards planted became badly mixed, which necessitated re-budding or top working over a good many trees, hence the nurserymen soon learned to avoid selecting budwood where they was any danger of getting the Australian type.

In spite of care, however, the nurserymen were still receiving complaints from planters that a certain percentage of so-called Australian Navels showed up in the stock purchased from them, and on examination it was found that certain trees, while not having all the traits of the Australian type, were decidedly of an inferior quality, which lead to the conclusion that possibly some buds were from sucker wood or water sprouts and that this caused the trees to be of inferior quality from the parent tree, for it was noted that these suckers or water sprouts, if allowed to mature in the tree, would always produce a rough, inferior fruit the first year or two they bore, although it usually improved as the growth advanced and became less vigorous.

This was no doubt the cause of the trouble, for it was noticed that the nurseryman, who was careful in the selection of buds, had less complaint about bad trees, although none escaped completely. No one at that time attributed the trouble to anything but careless selection of bud wood, either from sucker wood or trees of the Australian type, hence the nurseryman who personally selected his budwood from trees

Precocious rows of one-year-old Washington Navels, showing blooming and fruiting qualities.

known to be all right usually felt perfectly safe in taking budwood later, either from young orchards planted from his former selection or even from stock in the nursery row.

As time went on and citrus fruits attained larger prominence commercially it was seen that the yield was not what it should be. Growers found that there was always a certain percentage of trees that failed to produce a normal crop, or that produced rough inferior fruit, thus cutting down their average on the whole orchard both in quantity and quality. For a number of years this condition was attributed to either poor nursery stock, improper irrigation, cultivation or fertilization; but after a more careful investigation it was learned that there were certain trees in nearly every orchard that produced heavy crops of good quality fruit year after year, while others always bore light crops and still others that produced fruit of an inferior quality. Through the assistance of the Department of Agriculture a thorough investigation of the causes for this condition was made which showed that not only the Washington Navels, but all varieties of citrus fruits sported "off types" of inferior quality fruit and that often trees producing perfect fruit might have one limb or branch that produced either a poor quality of fruit or very little. This condition would continue year after year so that bud wood taken from that particular branch would produce fruit of like quality and quantity. Often these sport branches varied in growth and foliage. Whatever the variation, whether in fruit or foliage, buds taken from such wood are likely to produce trees of likely quality. This bud variation is particularly noticeable in Washington Navels and Valencia Late oranges and Eureka lemons, although it no doubt exists to a certain extent in all varieties of citrus fruit. Mr. A. D. Shamel, of the Department of Agriculture, in charge of fruit improvement investigations since 1909, says: "It may manifest itself in the habit of growth of the trees or their method of branching, the size, form, texture or the color of the foliage, or the form, color, texture, abundance, or scarcity of the fruit. Occasionally one tree grown from a single bud will develop several distinct strains of fruit. Frequently a single fruit or a branch bearing several fruits will be found on a tree having characteristics distinct from the fruit of the typical strain borne by the tree as a whole. Minor variations on fruit characteristics are very frequent occurrences."

From the knowlege thus gained in these investigations it is easy to see why nurserymen were continually receiving complaints about shy bearing trees and off types of fruit. To the casual observer it might appear strange that the deterioration was not greater, but it must be borne in mind that not all variations are downward or to inferior types. The investigations have not recorded the variations which showed improvement over the parent type and possibly it is not as great as the downward. In all these investigations the idea has been to eliminate the poorer strains and show best how to avoid future deteriorations, hence it is the duty of the nurserymen to select and propagate from those variations that give promise of being improvements over original types. The Thomson Improved, Golden Nugget and Buckeye Navels and

Original Washington Navel tree in Riverside

Navelencia are all sports or variations from the Washington Navel that gave promise of being improved in some particular over the original type. So in all varieties of citrus fruit, the perfect strains of today show a decided improvement over the original due to the nurseryman's effort to produce better and more perfect types of fruit, notwithstanding the fact that in the past they have been working more or less in the dark with reference to these bud variations. In recent years it has been the practice to select buds from those orchards that produced good crops of fruit as a whole and where there were no trees of the off or so-called Australian type; or, if there were any, to so mark them, so as to escape their use for purposes of propagation. In this way it was considered quite safe to take bud wood from such orchards even

One Million seed bed stock grown in the open nine months from planting.

though it was at the season of the year when there was no fruit on the trees.

From these facts it will be seen that it is hazardous to cut budwood from any tree without fruit to show the type and quality, and it is much more desirable, in fact it is the practice of the leading nurserymen, to select buds from trees or orchards having a performance record covering a period of from two to four or more years showing the trees to be consistent and regular bearers. In this way bud variation is overcome and the risk of planters getting trees that may prove untrue to type is reduced to a minimum.

In keeping performance records the orchard trees are each numbered, usually by the use of three sets of figures. The orchard is first divided into blocks of five or ten acres in each block, and numbered block one, two, three, etc. The rows are then numbered usually commencing at the irrigation head, for example, the eighth tree in the fourth row of block one would be numbered 1-4-8.

The fruit from each tree is picked and placed in separate boxes and a record made of the number of full boxes and an estimate of the partly filled boxes, or, if it is desired to be more exact, there are methods provided for weighing the fruit from each tree. By following this method for two or more years and comparing the production for each year, it can easily be determined which trees are profitable and those that are not. The latter trees should be worked over by top budding from budwood selected from the profitable producing trees.

BUDS FROM RECORD TREES

Buds selected from trees having a good performance record if taken when the fruit is still on the tree (so as to avoid getting wood from any sporting limbs that might be present) will produce trees showing little, if any, variation from the parent tree. The benefit to be derived from bud selection was recognized by the California Fruit Growers' Exchange, and a bud selection department was established under the management of the Fruit Growers' Supply Company, a subsidiary corporation, to carry on the work of selecting and selling bud wood from trees bearing good types of fruit and having a high performance record. These records are kept as elsewhere described, and the work is under the supervision of competent Exchange men so as to insure accuracy. The buds are also cut by experienced men, care being exercised to see that only fruiting wood is taken from the best trees. The buds from each tree are kept separate and given the number of the parent tree and they are delivered to the purchaser under that number. We keep all of these numbers separate in our nurseries and in delivering trees to our customers they come under the same tree numbers, so that if a purchaser gets trees marked "Tree No. 3002," he can go to the Fruit Growers' Supply Company's records and ascertain just what the parent tree record of production was.

do not suffer either from lack of water or cultivation. Trees that have been stunted for water usually show a lack of fibre roots, a condition that is not desirable in young stock and one that tends to make them much harder to start when transplanted. We take up our trees either balled or open roots, according to the wishes of our customers. Before starting to dig we cut back the tops to within about six or eight inches of the trunk. Too much foliage cannot be left or it will cause a greater evaporation than the roots can

A block of one hundred thousand one-year-old budded citrus trees.

TRAINING THE YOUNG BUDS

All of our trees are firmly staked as soon as the buds begin to grow and before the new growth has hardened, so that they can be tied up perfectly straight. The training of the young buds is given very close attention so as to insure straight stock. Every few days men go over the nursery taking off any suckers or sprouts that may appear and tying up such new growth as has been made since the preceding trip. When the trees have reached a heighth of thirty or more inches and the wood is well rounded out, they are topped at a uniform height of thirty inches and allowed to form a head. This tends to make the tree fill out and get more stocky, enabling it to withstand the wind much better. A low-headed tree also has the advantage of shading its own trunk from the sun's rays while it is young and tender and susceptible to sunburn..

During all the time our trees are growing in the nursery row we take particular pains to see that they stand. In balling extreme care is used in cutting out the ball so as not to disturb the root system contained therein. As soon as the ball is cut out it is placed in a burlap sack and firmly tied so that in handling the soil will not be shattered. As soon as this is done they are placed in the shade or taken to the lath house where they are wet down and heeled in wet shavings until wanted by the planter. We advise our customers to let us hold balled stock in the lath house for a few days after balling in order to give it a chance to recover from the shock of digging. This also gives the roots a chance to heel over and the tree is in condition to start right off growing as soon as set out in the orchard. This is especially advisable in late summer planting.

In taking up open root trees, it is necessary to use even more precaution than with balled ones. The soil is well irrigated before hand, so that all the fibre roots possible may be saved. By careful trenching on one side and cutting the tap root, then forcing the spade down on the opposite side, the tree is pried loose and the earth is shaken off the roots. As they are taken out the roots are covered with a wet cloth or burlap to protect them from the sun, and placed at the end of the rows where they are loaded in wagons for delivery to local customers, or taken to the packing house to be packed in moss and boxes for shipment. The roots on trees taken up in this manner are dipped in a mixture of earth and water of about the consistency of paint before they are packed in boxes or delivered to customers. This will cling to the roots and thoroughly protect them from wind and

location where the danger of damaging frosts is slight.

Citrus trees, especially lemons, should not be planted where the winter temperature reaches a minimum of 26 degrees or lower. Trees after reaching the age of four to six years will stand a temperature considerably lower than this without serious injury, but a temperature of 26 degrees for four hours or more will damage the fruit to the extent of reducing the owner's income to a point where it is not profitable to grow citrus fruits, and land in such localities had better be used for the more hardy fruits.

Standard commercial sizes of citrus nursery trees.
Left to right, 2 year buds caliper; 1—1 inch and up; 2—¾ to 1 inch; 3—⅝ to ¾. 1 year buds: 4—⅝ and up; 5—½ to ⅝; 6—⅜ to ½.

sun. We use the best sphagnum moss obtainable for packing and trees properly packed with it will keep in perfect condition for several months; in fact, we have had stock in transit for three months and it reached its destination in fine shape, and our customers advise us that it all grew, hence we do not hesitate to assure those at a distance that we can pack trees in this manner so that they will reach them in a satisfactory condition.

SELECTING GOOD CITRUS LAND

Too much stress cannot be placed on the importance of selecting a suitable location for the orchard. While citrus trees will grow under a variety of conditions, it does not by any means hold that they will bear profitable crops under all of them. Thousands of dollars have been lost to planters by trying to grow orchards where soil and weather conditions were not favorable. To gain maximum results a deep, well drained, soil should be selected and in a

The formation of the state is such that variations of climate occur quite frequently within short distances, and likewise, there are changes in character of soils so pronounced that it quite often happens that certain lands in a locality may be well adapted for citrus culture, while just a short distance away the soil or climatic conditions may not be desirable for their growth; hence, in choosing a location, be sure that these two essentials are right. It is far better to pay a thousand dollars an acre for desirable land than to undertake to raise an orchard on poor land even if given to you.

Water is the all important factor. It should not only be plentiful but the cost should be low enough to prevent the planter from having to stint his trees in order to make both ends meet. The most desirable lands being on the hill slopes or in protected valleys along the foothills, it follows that water for irrigation purposes is more expensive than for general farming, and usually less plentiful, and people looking for land for citrus planting should make sure that the water supply is sufficient for a mature orchard. As trees reach the bearing age they gradually require more water in order to support a crop.

Along the coast where the climate is tempered by the ocean breezes and occasional fogs it is estimated that an inch of water, continuous flow, is sufficient to properly irrigate seven or eight acres of orchard. This is assuming that the supply can be accumulated and taken at thirty or forty-day intervals; in other words, a party having forty acres of land with a water right of one inch to eight acres would be entitled to five inches continuous flow, or one hundred and fifty inches for twenty-four hours, if taken every thirty days; but as one hundred and fifty inches is usually more than can be handled to advantage on forty acres, fifty inches could be run for seventy-two hours, or twenty-five inches for one hundred and forty-four hours.

In the interior valleys where the temperature is higher and the humidity less it requires an inch of water to every three or four acres of orchard. The annual cost of water for a mature grove varies with local conditions, from $5.00 per acre in localities where water is more easily obtained, to as high as $40.00 per acres, where it has to be lifted an excessive height or carried in a long expensive ditch or pipe system. However, we do not consider this too expensive, provided all other conditions are ideal.

We would much prefer to pay $40.00 per acre for water on good rich land where heavy crops are assured and the danger of killing frosts is eliminated than to run the risk of losing a crop every few years on lands where the water was less expensive. We do not mean by this that all good citrus lands are expensive to irrigate or that cheap water indicates poor land. As stated above, water costs are regulated by local conditions and ideal lands are to be had in some localities where water is abundant and cheap.

PREPARING THE LAND FOR ORCHARD

Having selected the location, the next important problem is preparing for the new orchard. This is a matter that too many orchardists do not realize the importance of until later years when it is too late to correct their errors. By all means have the land in perfect condition both as to tilth and grade before starting to plant a tree. Better postpone planting

Lath house containing ten thousand balled trees ready for shipment.

two or three months, or even a year, rather than make the mistake of planting too soon.

If the land is uneven or rolling, engage a competent engineer to run levels, set grade stakes and locate the necessary pipe lines for irrigating. This will expedite the work of grading so that no unnecessary dirt will have to be moved, and when finished should lay so that every tree can be properly irrigated. On land nearly level it is often times advisable to plow furrows and run the water before starting to plant to be assured the grade is perfect. On lands where heavy fills are necessary this method is essential to insure against the uneven settling of unpacked soil in these places, as it often happens that regrading is necessary to fill up these depressions.

Being satisfied that the grading is complete, have the entire acreage plowed to a depth of eight or ten inches and thoroughly pulverized. A heavy drag or clod-smasher run over the ground will smooth it down and facilitate the staking process. It is usually best for those inexperienced in this work to engage a practical tree planter to lay off their ground and plant out the orchard. This insures straight rows and properly planted trees.

There are several different methods of planting,

Ten Acre Valencia orchard, 13 years planted to Teague trees, averaging 5661S packed boxes per annum for 11 years.

and we herewith illustrate the four systems used. The Square and Hexagonal, or Septuple, systems are the two most commonly used. In our opinion the Square method is the best, however, the latter can be used to advantage in some plantings.

The Square method gives more room for working among the trees, which is especially desirable after the trees reach maturity. At the age of six years the feeding roots of citrus trees planted twenty feet apart will occupy the entire space between the rows so that as far as space is concerned, there is no waste ground in planting by this method. It is a mistaken idea to plant trees too close, and in planting by the Hexagonal system we would advise its use as a means of giving the trees more room rather than to get more trees on the ground. If it is desired to get ninety trees per acre on the ground, which figures twenty-two feet apart each way by the Square method, it might be advisable to plant Hexagonal, which would make the distance twenty-three feet and six inches between trees, thus giving each tree an extra foot and a half more space.

Square System. The rows are laid off equal distances apart and the trees planted the same distance in the row, four trees forming a square. In laying out ground by this system parallel base lines are run on two sides of the tract. These lines must be perfectly straight and the same distance apart, the distance being governed by the size of the tract and the space left between the trees. For example, in planting trees twenty feet apart on a ten-acre tract, which is usually 660 feet square, the first base line would be laid off on one side of the tract and ten feet in from the property line, allowing this ten feet for a margin or turning row; the other base line would be run on the opposite side of the tract and the same distance in from the property line. This would make the two base lines 640 feet apart or just 32 twenty-foot space.

A 660-foot wire with buttons or cloth securely fastened every twenty feet, beginning ten feet from the end, is used for laying out both the base lines and the rows. When properly stretched along the first base line, stakes are set at each button to mark where the rows will come, the first stake being ten feet in from property line. The second base line is run and staked in the same manner, taking care that they are the same distance apart at all points. This can be done by stretching the wire from each end of the first base line, and at right angles to it, being careful that the first button is held exactly at the stake on the base line each time. The button on the opposite end of the chain will be the line for the second base line. Mark these two points and then run the second base line. With these two base lines run and marked, the line is then used to mark off the rows, starting at either side at the first row and stretching the line so that the last button on each end is at the base line stake on that end. Make the line fast and proceed to set stakes at each of the buttons between the base lines, then move to the next stake and proceed across the tract. If care has been used in getting the line straight each time and the end buttons to the base line stakes the rows will line perfectly in all directions.

Triangular or Alternate System. Ground is staked as in Square method, except that a second line of stakes is required one way half way between the rows and every alternate tree is planted in this row. The only advantage of this system is that it gives the trees a little more room; this is, however, offset by the disadvantage in working between the trees the narrow way. The number of trees to the acre is the same as by the Square method.

Quincunx System. The ground is laid out as in the Square system and another stake set in the center of each square making a double set orchard. This method is only practiced where it is desired to have two sets of trees on the same ground with the idea of taking out one or the other when they begin to crowd.

Hexagonal or Septuple System. In this system six trees form a hexagon and enclose a seventh. Three trees form an equilateral triangle. In laying out the ground for this method of planting the simplest arrangement to use is an equilateral triangle form made of 1x3 inch material the length it is desired to set the trees apart. Then run two base lines similar to the Square method, excepting that they should be at right angles to each other. This will give a straight row across one side and one end of the tract. Only one line is staked, the other being simply a guiding line to keep the rows straight with the property. In staking the one base line, first determine the distance in from the property line it is desired to plant the first row each way, the base line being the first row on one side and the right angle guide line being the first row the other way, then set the first stake one half the dis-

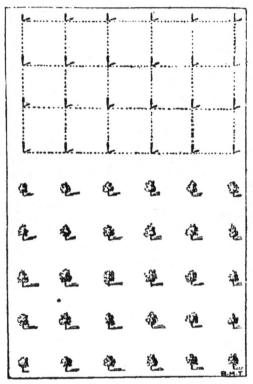

Square system

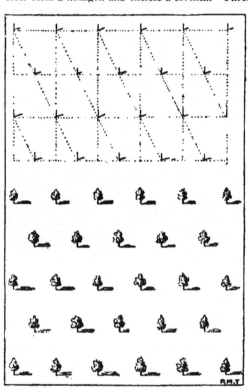

Triangular or alternate system

tance it is desired to plant the trees from the junction of these two lines. If planting twenty feet apart this first stake should be ten feet from the junction, and if twenty-two feet apart set the stake eleven feet in.

After this line is staked use the triangle form above mentioned, setting one point at the first stake, the second point on the guide line, and the third point will indicate the third row of trees. Set stakes at the second and third points. With these points established the triangle can be worked either way. If working down the guide line simply turn the form

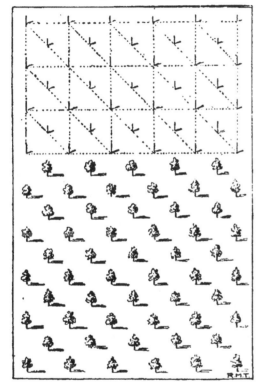

Quincunx system

over, being careful to keep points two and three at the stakes, point one will then be facing in the opposite direction, set stake at number one and turn form again with point two on the guide line and set stakes at point two and then follow this process across the field, thus staking three rows by using rows two and three for guide lines the operators can work back to the base line, but only one row can be staked as points one and two of the form will have to be placed at the stakes on rows two and three, but two rows can be staked from the base line each time. Three men will be required to operate this plan of staking, and if care is used the trees should line perfectly, provided of course the land is on a uniform grade.

If uneven or rolling land is to be staked off a line similar to that described under the Square system can be used, but there will have to be two sets of end buttons, as it will be seen from the illustration that the rows alternate, also the two parallel base lines would have to be double staked.

After the ground is staked off in the manner described each stake will indicate the point at which a tree will be set. In order to preserve this location while digging the holes a planting board is used and the ground is double staked. For the purpose of making its use more clearly understood we give an illustration of the planting board.

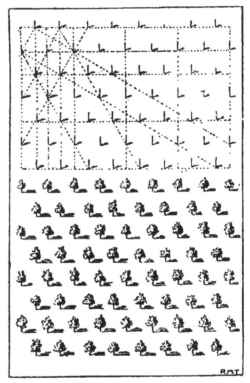

Hexagonal or septuple system

Use a piece of 1x4 pine, 4 feet in length, cut notches A and B one inch square in each end as illus-

trated. In the exact center cut notch C 1½ inches square, or larger if the diameter of the trees to be planted require it. In double staking place notch C over the tree stake each time, being careful that the stake comes in the center of the notch. With the board firmly held in this position drive stakes in notches A and B, remove the board and pull up the tree stake at C, and dig the hole. In planting the tree replace the board in same position holding the trunk of the tree in notch C until the soil is filled in around it.

In digging the holes be careful not to disturb the two stakes set with the planting board or it will be impossible to get the tree accurately set. The holes should be dug 18 to 20 inches in diameter and about the same depth. Open root trees require a somewhat larger hole than balls. It is not advisable to dig the hole much deeper than necessary to hold the ball or roots, as there is danger of the tree settling if too deep, and it is never best to have them any deeper than they stood in the nursery. If holes are too deep fill up to the required depth and pack firmly. When it is necessary to dig deeper holes or blast in order to break up hard pan or heavy clay sub-soil, water should be run before planting so as to thoroughly settle the earth before planting the tree. The following table will show the number of trees to the acre by the Square, Quincunx, and Hexagonal, or Septuple system:

Distance Apart	Square	Hexagonal or Septuple	Quincunx
10 feet	436	500	831
12 feet	303	347	571
14 feet	222	255	415
16 feet	170	195	313
18 feet	134	154	247
20 feet	108	126	199
22 feet	90	103	173
24 feet	76	96	137
30 feet	48	56	83

Note.—In giving the distances of trees of the quincunx, the fifth or central tree is not taken into account.

In determining the proper distance to plant citrus trees their habits and growth should be considered, always keeping in mind the fact that it is better to seemingly give the trees a little too much room rather than too little. Unlike planting ordinary farm crops where a mistake can be rectified the following year, a citrus orchard is planted but once in a lifetime. Remember that sunlight and air are essential elements in the production of all fruits and if trees are so crowded that their branches touch, very little fruit can be expected excepting in their tops where the required light and air is available. The lower limbs and sides of the tree where the bulk of the fruit should be produced remain barren.

A six-year-old Marsh Seedless pomelo grove planted to Teague trees yielding 5 to 6 boxes per tree.

Our recommendation for planting the different varieties would be for Washington Navels and other varieties of similar growth, 22 feet apart by the Square or 24 feet by the Hexagonal method. The Washington Navel is not usually a rapid growing tree excepting when planted on light alluvial soils, and in such locations we would advise planting a little further apart.

Valencia Lates should be planted at least 24 feet apart on the Square or 26 feet on the Hexagonal method. They are vigorous growing trees, and to secure the best results when they reach maturity they should have plenty of room.

Lemon trees are fully as vigorous as Valencias, but due to the necessity of constant pruning they do not usually make quite as tall a tree; however, the production is heavier, and the pruning having a tendency to cause the branches to spread out they should be given fully as much room as the Valencia. The necessity for almost constant work in cultivating, irrigating, picking, hauling and pruning make it essential that ample room be allowed.

Pomelos should be planted the same distance apart

Eureka lemon orchard planted to Teague trees producing $8.50 per tree gross for seven years.

as Valencias or lemons. They are vigorous growing trees and require plenty of room if maximum results are to be expected. If crowded the fruit will be small and inferior.

Satsumas, Mexican Limes, Kumquats and other slow growing varieties may be planted as close as 16 feet apart.

SELECTING GOOD TREES

By all means plant good trees. The first cost of a tree is a small item compared with the expense of bringing it to maturity. The cost of nursing along an inferior tree to the age of maturity is vastly more than that of bringing a thrifty vigorous growing tree to the same age. Poor trees rarely make a first class orchard, while good trees properly cared for seldom fail. Patronize a reliable nurseryman whose reputation for supplying good stock is unquestioned and whose experience in citrus culture will enable him to give valuable advice and instructions in planting and caring for orchards. Should mistakes occur, or for any reason the trees fail to grow satisfactorily, a responsible nurseryman can be depended on to make good any errors or omissions on his part. Trees secured from reliable sources usually give satisfaction and cause for complaint is rare.

Whether to plant balled or open root trees depends largely on the season of the year the planting is done and nature of soil in which trees are to be planted. For late summer planting, or where the soil is inclined to be heavy, we advise the use of balled trees. These are taken out of the nursery with 40 to 75 pounds of earth on the roots (depending on size of tree) and sacked and tied so that the root system contained in the ball is not disturbed, and if handled with reasonable care and properly watered when planted the trees rarely ever wilt.

Trees handled in this way can be transplanted at almost any time of year with satisfactory results. Open root trees require more careful handling, but if planted early before the weather gets too warm and on light or sandy soil good results will be attained. In taking up trees in this manner all the soil is taken off the roots, care being used to prevent their being exposed to wind or sun while being prepared for packing. Damp moss is used for packing, and when properly packed trees handled in this manner will keep in perfect condition for two or three months. We make shipment of trees packed in this manner to Mexico, South America, South Africa, China and Japan, and they always arrive in good condition.

PLANTING BALLED TREES

First of all handle them carefully. The purpose of balling is to get an undisturbed root system. By rough handling the roots are jarred loose or broken off in the ball and the benefit of balling is lost. Better plant a properly handled open root tree than a roughly handled balled one. Never carry a balled tree by the trunk or top, always lift it by the ball, either by placing the hands under the bottom or by grasping the sack at the base of the trunk. We try to see that trees are handled in this manner at the nursery, and if planters will see that their employees are just as careful there will be less cause for complaint.

Having received the trees at the place of planting, see that they are not unduly exposed during the planting. Only such trees as are to be immediately planted should be distributed in the field. The remainder should be kept in the shade and sprinkled if necessary to prevent the balls from drying out. We have seen trees set in the field for a day or two before being planted and all grow, but it is a dangerous practice, especially if the weather is warm or windy, and the trees receiving this additional shock cannot be expected to do as well as those properly handled.

In setting the tree try and get it as near the same depth as it stood in the nursery. Usually the top of the ball should be about one inch below the level of the ground, this allows for about that much loose soil that is taken off in balling the trees. As trees usually settle some after the water is applied, it is best to set them just a little shallow rather than too deep. Having gotten the tree in the hole, see that the trunk and top are perpendicular before filling in the soil. It is customary for one man to hold the tree in place while one or two others fill up the hole. It is advisable to use good top soil for this rather than that taken from the bottom of the hole.

When the hole is about two-thirds filled, cut the string at the top and turn down the sack, then finish filling the hole. This allows the sack to quickly rot and prevents the possibility of afterwards hooking on to the sack with hoe or cultivator and disturbing the tree. Do not pack the soil by hand or foot as it is being placed around the ball. Firm it just sufficient to hold the tree in place. The water will settle it much better and more thoroughly if left in this way.

Water should be run as soon as possible after planting. While balled trees will stand some time without watering, it is best to settle the soil around the ball within a few hours after planting, especially if the weather is warm. After watering and before the soil is thoroughly set, go over the orchard and straighten up any trees that may have settled out of line. After straightening up the tree fill in with dry soil and hoe as soon as dry enough to prevent cracking or drying out around the tree. Water thoroughly again in ten days or two weeks, after which time the trees should not require irrigation for from three weeks to thirty days, depending on weather conditions. In planting in the interior valleys during the summer months it is advisable to irrigate every ten days for at least six weeks after planting.

PLANTING OPEN ROOT TREES

As stated elsewhere, it is necessary to use much more care in handling open root trees, as it is absolutely essential that the roots never be allowed to dry out. When planting trees dug in this way never take but one tree at a time out of the box or package in which they are received, then immediately plant it using moist soil to fill in the hole. Never use hot dry dirt or disaster will follow.

The man holding the tree in place should spread out the lateral roots as the hole is filled up so that they will be as near in their natural position as possible. If planted in warm weather, water should be immediately applied. The best results can be obtained by using a tank wagon for watering the first time, and if the soil is inclined to be dry fill the hole with water before filling in the earth, or as it is being filled in. This will completely saturate and settle the soil around the roots. If it is not practical to use a tank wagon, or if irrigation water is available, have the water running down the rows as the trees are being set, and never plant more than one or two trees ahead of the water.

In using this method, it is best to double stake the ground so that a furrow can be run between the stakes before the holes are dug. This will facilitate getting the water to the trees more quickly. Water should be again applied as in planting balled trees, excepting that the ground around the trees must be more closely watched than with balled stock, and if it shows any sign of drying out or cracking apply the second irrigation more quickly.

CARE OF THE ORCHARD

The success of all agricultural and horticultural pursuits depends largely on the care and attention given them, and in none is this more pronounced than in citrus culture. Citrus trees will survive under most trying conditions of neglect and abuse, but to attain any degree of success in the production of profitable crops, one must give them good care, which means proper irrigation, sufficient cultivation and enough fertilization to keep them well supplied with plant food. The latter applies more particularly to bearing trees.

The most of our California soils contain sufficient plant food so that fertilization is not absolutely necessary for the first two or three years, but a little fertilizer applied each year after the trees are planted will tend to keep up the fertility of the soil and often times adds to the vigor of the tree.

allowed to go just a little short of water, it will tend to send its feeding roots deeper where the moisture is more uniform and thus enable it to better withstand the summer heat. One can go to extremes both ways in the matter of irrigation, either of which is dangerous to the future welfare of the orchard, but it is safe to say that whenever the trees show the least signs of wilting they should be irrigated.

The method of irrigation most generally used is

Irrigating a hillside citrus fruit orchard by contour furrowing.

It is impossible to lay down any hard and fast rule as to the proper amount, time and manner of applying water in the irrigation of citrus orchards. These matters depend largely on the nature of the soil and climatic condition of the locality where the planting is done. After the trees are established it is not usually necessary to irrigate oftener than once in every thirty days or six weeks, excepting on very light sandy soils where it is sometimes necessary to irrigate every three or four weeks, especially during the warmest part of the summer. In our opinion it is more dangerous to irrigate young trees too much rather than too little. The over irrigation tends to bring the fibre roots close to the surface where the least warm weather and drying out of the surface soil will cause the tree to wilt, whereas if the tree is

known as the furrow system. In young trees one furrow is made on each side of the row eight to sixteen inches from the tree, and the water is run until the soil is well saturated up to the tree. On newly planted stock, it is sometimes advisable to hoe the soil away and allow the water to come even closer than this in order to be assured that the moisture will reach every part of the root system, but in no case should the soil be hoed away so as to allow the water to stand around the trunk of the tree. As the trees get older the furrows are run further away from the trees and in soils where the moisture does not spread rapidly, it is advisable to run cross furrows on each side of the trees and run the water into these from the main ones. After the second year, two furrows should be run on each side of the trees and later, as the feeding roots reach the center of the space between the rows, the entire space should be furrowed out and irrigated. Care should be exercised at all times to see that the water is run a sufficient length of time to thoroughly wet the sub-soil, thus enabling the root system to stay well below the surface. In light sandy soils, the water will sub-irrigate sufficiently while running through the rows, or at least within 30 minutes to one hour after reaching the ends, but in the heavier soils it requires a much smaller stream to each row and the time required to thoroughly wet the sub-soil varies from one half day to as much as three or four days, the latter time only being required on the very heaviest clay soils where there is a considerable slope to the land.

What is known as the basin system is used on very light level lands. This method should never be applied only where the soil is sufficiently porous, so that the water will not stand in the basins but a few minutes after they are filled. In this system, ridges are run both ways, dividing the land off into blocks or squares, usually one tree to a square, and a ditch or furrow is made between the rows to convey the water to the squares. As each square is filled the water is shut off and carried to the next, usually beginning at the lower end of the orchard and working up to the head. We do not recommend this system excepting where the soil is so loose and level that the furrow system is impracticable.

Citrus trees do not usually require irrigation during the winter months. The rainfall generally is sufficient for their winter requirements. However, it sometimes happens that through lack of rain they require a light irrigation or two during the winter or spring. Three to five irrigations during the summer months are the average requirements necessary to keep a mature orchard in proper condition.

The proper cultivation of the orchard is equally as important as the irrigation and the full value of the irrigation cannot be conserved if the cultivation is delayed or improperly done. The requirements of the different soils vary as to time and manner of cultivation. A light sandy soil can be worked in about 24 hours after the water is shut off, while the heavier clay soils should be allowed to dry from two to five days, depending on the weather before cultivating. On soils of this nature it is advisable to fill in the furrows with a harrow just as soon as the surface shows signs of baking or crusting over. By doing this the cultivation can be delayed for two or three days or until the soil below is sufficiently dried so that it will not stick together or turn up in solid masses. Avoid cultivating heavy soil when it is too wet, as it not only dries out much faster, but makes it more difficult to work in the future.

The main idea in cultivation is to pulverize the surface soil, so as to form a mulch fine enough to prevent the sub-soil from drying out. If left loose and cloddy much of the good is lost and irrigation will be necessary again in a much shorter time. It is customary to cultivate the ground from two to eight times after each irrigation, going in a different direction each time, so as to thoroughly pulverize it on all sides of the trees. Each cultivation should be a little deeper than the preceding one so that when the work is completed there will be a mulch of fine soil from 4 to 6 inches deep. By starting shallow and going a little deeper each time it tends to pulverize the soil better and in heavy land prevents it from breaking up in large clods. These cultivations should not follow each other closely, but at intervals of from two to four days after each two cultivations.

During the winter months, if it is desired to keep the orchard clean, the ground should be cultivated after each rain and at this time of year it is not as necessary to pulverize the soil; in fact it is better to leave it a little rough so that the rains will have a chance to soak in.

The practice of sowing winter cover crops or of leaving the natural vegetation grow during the winter months, is being quite extensively followed now, and as most of our California soils are deficient in humus, it gives quite satisfactory results, where properly handled in the spring. In following this plan it is always advisable to leave the orchard furrowed out for irrigation so that in case of a shortage of rain during the winter or spring, an irrigation can be given the trees whenever necessary. The cover crop should be turned under with a plow as early in the spring as possible. It is not advisable to plow or cultivate very deep just before or during blooming time, and if the cover crop cannot be plowed in before this, it is better to wait until after the fruit is set and then work it up with a disc, but in this case it will be necessary to keep the ground well watered so that the trees will not suffer during the blooming period, as at this time the energy of the tree is taxed to the limit, and the root system needs all the help possible to support the top in its effort to set a crop.

FERTILIZATION

The many different soil conditions in California makes it impossible to lay down any set rules for this most important factor, but it is a matter that should have the attention of the planter before the orchard begins to show that it is in the need of plant food. It is much more difficult and costly to bring an orchard back into condition, once it has suffered from the lack of fertilizer, than it is to keep it thrifty by adding plant food as the available supply is being consumed.

The three chemicals necessary in the soil to sustain plant life are nitrogen, phosphoric acid, and potash. All our soils contain these ingredients, but not always in available forms or sufficient quantities to grow trees successfully, and never is the supply great enough to last indefinitely, hence sooner or later the artificial appliaction of plant food must be resorted to.

It is best to start in while the trees are young and

A citrus tree budded to twenty-two different varieties.

fertilize enough to keep the fertility of the soil from becoming exhausted. This can be done by growing cover crops of legumes, or supplying barn-yard manures or commercial fertilizers. The legumes most generally used are peas, vetch, fenuegreek and the clovers, the bitter clover (Melilotus Indica) being the most popular on account of its rank growth. As all legumes gather nitrogen from the air and store it in the stalk and roots of the plant, they are much more desirable as a cover crop than any other form of vegetation. The amount of nitrogen derived from a good cover crop together with its value in adding humus to the soil makes it one of the cheapest ways of fertilizing. The value of a cover crop depends largely on the amount of growth it makes and the manner in which it is turned under in the spring. A large part of the value of any cover crop, manure or fertilizer is lost if it is left on top of the ground. It must be placed where the feeding roots of the tree can reach it. It must be remembered that a certain amount of plant food is taken out of the ground by the cover crop and unless it is all turned under so that the tree can get the full benefit of it, the plant food returned to the soil may not exceed that consumed.

Barnyard manure is considered the best for citrus trees and careful experiments made with it show more satisfactory results than with any other method of fertilizing. Unfortunately the supply is so limited that it is not always possible to get a sufficient amount to properly fertilize any considerable acreage. On bearing trees 10 to 15 tons to the acre should be applied every other year.

Bean straw and alfalfa are also valuable fertilizers, but can only be used when a surplus of feed brings the price within reach of the orchardist for fertilizing purposes.

In using manure, much better results are obtained

by plowing very deep furrows on each side of the trees and placing the manure therein, then fill in the furrows and allow it to decay. This makes it available as a plant food much more quickly than by the old method of broad-casting it on the surface and plowing or discing it in.

There are a number of good commercial fertilizers put out by the different firms engaged in that business, and the use of these gives very satisfactory results, especially where used in connection with either cover crops or manure. On young trees, three to five pounds per tree is used and as the orchard reaches full bearing age, from 1,000 to 2,500 pounds per acre is applied. Commercial fertilizer should be drilled in to a depth of from 4 to 6 inches to get best results. In sowing it on the surface and attempting to cultivate it in, as much as 25 or 50% is lost by wind and sun before it can be worked down to where it is available to the tree.

The most successful orchardists are those who use plenty of fertilizers and apply them properly. The application of fertilizer in insufficient quantities or by improper methods is money thrown away. It has been said that for every dollar's worth of fertilizer properly applied, the orchardist may reasonably expect ten dollars in return. This may be putting it a little strong, but we do know that it pays to fertilize.

PRUNING THE ORANGE

Orange trees require very little pruning to keep them in proper shape as their natural inclination is to form a uniform and well balanced head. During the first three or four years the only pruning necessary is to cut out interfering branches, sucker growth, and shorten in such limbs as may have a tendency to throw the tree out of balance. In pruning, always use sharp tools and avoid making rough, uneven cuts. For light pruning use hand shears having the blade ground as thin as is safe, to avoid breaking. This will enable the operator to do good clean work with little or no bruising or splitting of the limbs. For the heavier work the long handled shears can be used, but we much prefer using a good pruning saw wherever the limbs are too large to be easily cut with the hand shears. In shortening in limbs, always aim to cut to a joint and where a limb is to be taken out entirely, be sure to cut close and avoid leaving a stump to sucker and sap the vitality of the tree. On all cuts such as it might be necessary to make with a saw, it is advisable to use some kind of paint or wax to keep out the moisture and prevent decay. Whatever is used for this purpose, it should be of such consistency that it will completely seal up the cut, or it may as well not be used.

As the trees develop, all dead limbs should be cut out together with such sucker growth as may appear and any other limbs that may clog the center or inside of the tree. The main idea being to have the center comparatively open and the outside fairly compact. By following this method, the bearing surface of the tree is doubled and at the same time the accumulation of dead wood is reduced to a minimum. Dead wood is due to an overcrowded condition of the branches and if this is corrected, it lessens the amount of dead wood. Above all things never clip or shear orange trees like a hedge plant, as this tends to produce a thick mass of short branches that will make the top so dense that the necessary sunlight and air cannot properly penetrate it. To the eye, a tree should present a compact mass of foliage but it should not be dense. If it is necessary to prune off limbs from the outside, cut them back to where they branch, preferably cutting to a branch having an upward tendency. All citrus trees are headed low and as the limbs on budded varieties have a tendency to droop, it is customary to allow the branches to hang down, the idea being to prune off just enough to prevent the fruit from brushing on the ground.

It is not necessary to prune orange trees oftener than once a year, although it adds to their vigor if all suckers or water sprouts are kept off, as they appear, or at least if they are taken off once between prunings. The customary time for pruning bearing orchards is in the spring just after the crop is picked.

PRUNING THE LEMON

Lemon trees require much more vigorous pruning than the orange and to get satisfactory results this work should commence the first year after planting. The tendency is for the limbs to grow long and irregular and if allowed to go unrestricted the tree will present a mass of long whip like branches, the fruit being more or less on the ends of these where it is easily whipped off or scarred and bruised by the winds. Lemons are also more inclined to send out suckers and water sprouts, and these must be kept pruned out. By starting while the tree is young and keeping the heavy growth checked, the tendency will be to develop more fruit wood and as the tree begins to devote more of its energy toward the production of fruit, it will be less inclined to make the vigorous rampant growth noted in the younger stock. It therefore follows that care must be exercised to cut out as little of this fruiting wood as possible and to this end the operator must learn to distinguish between the two. Sucker wood can readily be distinguished by its rank and sappy growth; the pith or soft tissue in the center of the limb is also much larger than in the fruit wood.

The limbs designed to make up the frame-work of the top should be well distributed so as to form a well shaped head and shortened back from time to time, so as to give them strength to carry the fruit of later years. The tops should be left somewhat more open than on oranges, and where clumps of growth come out from the ends of limbs shortened back, they should be thinned out and only those left that are necessary to shape up the top.

The vigorous growth of lemon trees makes it necessary to prune them two or three times a year especially while they are young. This makes each pruning less severe than would be necessary if it were left to be done only once a year, and the result to the tree is much more satisfactory. Lemon trees are headed at about the same height as orange trees and the same general rule as to allowing the branches to reach the ground applies. These lower limbs protect the trunk of the tree from the sun and also shade the ground around the tree. Having the trees headed low is also an advantage when it comes to gathering the fruit, as much of it can be gathered without the use of a step ladder.

STANDARD VARIETIES OF ORANGES

WASHINGTON NAVEL

Fruit. The Washington Navel stands at the head of California oranges. Fruit large to very large; peel invariably smooth and thick, rendering it of good productive quality; color a pronounced orange yellow; fruit marked at the blossom end with a small but irregular and secondary orange, from which it takes the name of "Navel"; fruit seedless and free from "rag"; flesh crisp and sweet, with abundant juice possessing a flavor peculiarly its own; shipping qualities of the best, "standing up" under long-distance shipments and yet maintaining its fine eating values.

Washington Navel orange

Tree. Of a rather moderate growth with small or no thorns and somewhat umbrageous in character with full rounded top; foliage a dark glossy green liberally furnished; in California a strong and regular bearer, often producing fruit the second year in orchard from the nursery rows.

History. This fruit was introduced into the United States in 1870 by the Federal Department of Agriculture under the name of the Bahia orange. Of the trees propagated by the Department two were sent to Mrs. L. C. Tibbets of Riverside in 1873; an event that can truthfully be said to constitute the founding of the orange industry in California. Originally the fruit was known as the Riverside Navel, but as it became known in other localities, the name was changed to Washington Navel, in honor of the Federal Capitol from which it was first sent out. The original two trees are still alive. One was transplanted in 1913, with the assistance of the late Colonel Roosevelt, to the court of the Riverside Mission Inn Hotel; the other still stands at the head of Magnolia avenue. Of this tree we show an illustration on another page of this book.

VALENCIA LATE

Fruit. Owing to its season, which extends from May to November, this variety is second only to the Washington Navel in commercial importance. The fruit is of medium size, slightly oval; color a good orange yellow; peel thin, smooth and of good protective quality; flesh of good grain with abundant juice of fine citrus flavor; practically seedless; shipping quality of the very best. The Valencia Late is the best summer shipping orange known to commerce, and coming into market at a season of the year when all other varieties have been disposed of, is essentially in a class by itself and exempt from competition.

Valencia Late orange

Tree. Splendid form and of vigorous upright growth, attaining to great size much like the seedling type of an earlier period of the citrus industry; almost thornless; its extensive planting can be commended on good citrus lands that are reasonably free from late biting frosts.

History. This fruit is a synonym of Hart's Late and Hart's Tardiff, and was introduced into California from Florida in the early seventies. Among our earlier experiences with citrus culture, we recall an orchard planted to Hart's Tardiff trees, which on coming into bearing developed a number of trees untrue to name. These we budded to Valencia Lates, which on coming into bearing, fruit and habit of trees were identical with the Hart's Tardiff.

THOMSON IMPROVED NAVEL

Fruit. The Year Book of the Department of Agriculture for 1911 gives the following description: Form slightly oblong; size above medium to large; cavity small, surface smooth; stem slender; color orange yellow, reddening somewhat after picking; peel relatively smooth, rather closely adherent, usually thin and rather tender; segments 10 to 12, irregular in size with open center; flesh, rich yellow to deep orange in color, translucent, moderately tender; not very abundant; seedless; flavor sweet, sprightly, pleasant; quality good, but not equal to the Washington Navel, but it reaches full maturity about one month earlier than that variety.

Continued on page 28

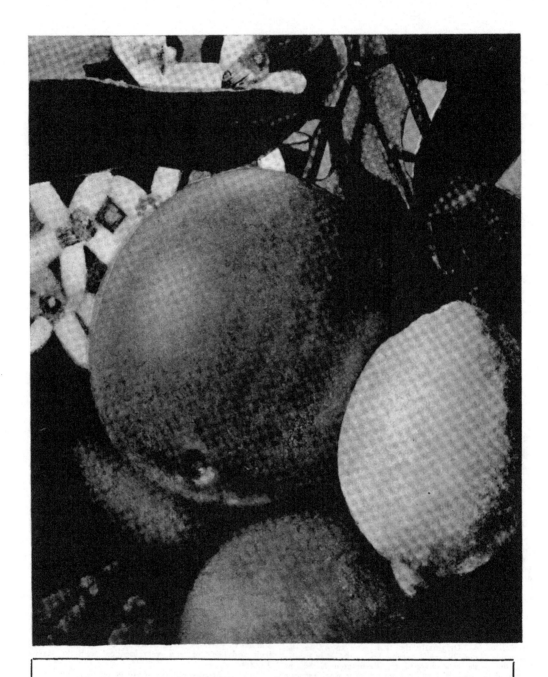

THE TWO GREAT FAVORITES

The two fruits that stand out supreme in California citrus culture are the Washington Navel orange and the Eureka lemon. The former finds its greatest development under California conditions while the latter not only luxuriates with us but originated in this State. Both are an ornament to horticulture and fruits of great economic value, which have added much to the horticultural wealth of the State. The tendency of these varieties to "sport" has caused a wide variation in the productiveness of the trees and the quality of the fruit, due to so called "off types." Bud selection gives promise of corecting this tendency so that both varieties will not only be more prolific but the quality of the fruit will be better and more uniform. For the Teague Nurseries have grown trees of the best types of both varieties which at the present time are being grown from selected buds from only record bearing trees, thus assuring the planter trees that will be uniform bearers of high quality fruit.

LEADERS IN THEIR CLASS

Two fruits of later introduction than the Washington Navel are the Valencia Late orange and Marsh Seedless pomelo. Indeed it can almost be said that these combined with the Washington Navel orange and the Eureka lemon constitute the four pillars supporting the California citrus industry. These two varieties of oranges constitute fully 70 percent of the total trees in orchard form, while Marsh Seedless pomelos and Eureka lemons are easily the most popular in their respective classes. The Valencia Late orange makes the supply of fresh oranges continuous throughout the year. Its good keping qualities combined with its excellent flavor places it in the front rank as the ideal summer orange. The same may be said of the Marsh Seedless pomelo as the fruit will stay on the tree from one season to the next without deterioration.

Tree. In habit and appearance very much like the Washington Navel; a good grower, strong foliage and well branched.

History. This fruit takes its name from that of the man (Mr. A. C. Thomson) on whose grounds it was first observed. Its origin from a scientific point of view was a matter of much speculation in the early days of the citrus industry in California; but of late years it is quite generally conceded that it took its inception as a bud sport of the Washington Navel, rather than through any process or manipulation of buds.

Navelencia orange

NAVELENCIA

Fruit. In appearance much like the Thomson Navel, being of good size and shape; peel of fine grain and rather thin; flesh melting to the taste and reasonably free from "rag"; juice abundant and of good flavor; shipping qualities up to standard. Season, January to June.

Tree. Of an unbrageous habit with fine symmetrical top; possesses small thorns; foliage dark green and glossy; an early and good bearer, often yielding fruit the second year from the bud.

History. The claim that it is a cross between Thomson Navel and Valencia Late is hardly tenable; it probably is a variation in the regular Navel type of sufficient importance to give it specific rank. Not extensively cultivated as a commercial sort.

PAPER RIND ST. MICHAELS

Fruit. Rather small, round, solid and heavy; peel smooth, thin and of fine texture; color yellow verging to a lemon shade; membranes thin; grain of fine texture; juice abundant; flavor sweet and sprightly; good shipping quality. Season, April to June.

Tree. Strong and upright grower; medium thorny; a good bearer. St. Michael trees in the Azores, in sheltered situations, have been known to bear from 15,000 to 20,000 fruits in a single year.

History. One of the oldest varieties in cultivation in the Mediterranean countries and in the Azores, where it has long been a favorite. First planted in California in the early stages of the exploitation and development of the citrus industry.

MEDITERRANEAN SWEET

Fruit. Medium to large; shape oval; color a rich orange yellow; peel rather heavy and of good protective quality; flesh of good grain and orange yellow in color; flavor sweet and aromatic; a good shipping variety; season between Washington Navel and Valencia, usually from April to July.

Mediterranean Sweet orange

Tree. A good bearer and vigorous grower inclined to a spreading habit but not attaining great size; practically thornless; will stand a slightly colder temperature than some of the other sorts; at one time extensively planted in Southern California, but of late years planted sparingly.

History. Of European extraction and first introduced and disseminated in California by A. T. Garey in the late seventies and early eighties.

JOPPA

Fruit. Good size and highly colored when fully matured; has a smooth thin rind; flesh sweet and full of juice, very little rag and nearly seedless. Ripens in April but will stay on the tree as late as July.

Tree. Very vigorous and an upright grower, very much resembling the Valencia Late and quite thornless.

History. Introduced from Joppa, Palestine.

HOMOSASSA

Fruit. Round, medium to large in size. Peel smooth and thin; color orange yellow; flesh somewhat coarse but remarkably free from rag; flavor sprightly and of excellent quality; ripens early but does not drop.

Tree. Of medium growth but of somewhat spreading habit; quite prolific.

History. A Florida seedling originating in the grove of Hon. Mr. Yulee at Homosassa, Florida.

RUBY BLOOD

Fruit. Of medium size and round in shape; peel thin and inclined to be tough; pulp melting, juicy and of a rich acidulous flavor; flesh a ruby red as the fruit fully matures, showing through the peel, giving it a reddish blush on the outside; a fruit of prime quality in its class.

Tree. Nearly thornless, a good grower and prolific bearer; habit symmetrical and beautiful to the eye.

History. An imported variety, undoubtedly from some of the Mediterranean citrus districts. Introduced into Florida by General Sanford, from whence it undoubtedly found its way to California.

MALTA BLOOD

Fruit. Medium size, oval, of fine texture and flavor. Pulp streaked and mottled with a blood red and almost seedless. Peel has a reddish blush giving it an attractive appearance. Ripens at about the close of the Navel season.

Tree. Inclined to be of a dwarf habit with a peculiar character of growth making it very easy to distinguish from other varieties.

History. Introduced into California from Florida and probably brought there from the Mediterranean districts.

Ruby Blood orange

NEW AND RARE VARIETIES OF ORANGES

LUE GIM GONG

Fruit. Good commercial size of the Valencia type, ripens about the same time but will hang on the tree for two, and even three years, and still maintain its color and good eating qualities. Color a deep orange red; skin smooth, flesh deep orange, very juicy and free from rag. The flavor is a rich blending of sweet and sub-acid, and when fully ripe its delicious quality is unsurpassed. Almost seedless. Its keeping qualities are such that it will make a very desirable orange for shipping.

Tree. Very vigorous but inclined to be more spreading than the Valencias. A heavy and regular bearer; said to be very hardy and not easily damaged by cold.

History. A hybrid, propagated by a Mr. Lue Gim Gong of De Land, Florida, from seed secured by polinization of Hart's Late and Mediterranean Sweet.

GOLDEN NUGGET NAVEL

Fruit. Medium to large, solid and of good shape; peel thin, more so than that of the Washington Navel, of fine texture, surface being smooth to the touch, and of good color; flesh exceptionally free from rag and seedless; flavor of the best with abundant juice; a good shipper. Season February to May.

Tree. Somewhat individual by reason of its exceptionally dark green foliage, abundant lateral, or fruiting branches, and fine symmetrical appearance; foliage is more lanceolate than that of the Washington Navel, and in color a shade darker, not quite so broad nor apparently quite so thick or leathery; wood growth, particularly the younger branches, more slender and willowy.

History. A variation or "sport" originated in our orchards some years ago, which appealed so strongly as to its economic importance that we have taken buds from the parent tree and perpetuated the strain under the name of "Golden Nugget Navel." Possessing real merit, it is worthy of trial culture.

Golden Nugget Navel orange

GOLDEN BUCKEYE NAVEL

Fruit. The feature that distinguishes it from all other varieties of Navel is a series of ridges of a deeper orange color on the peel, which is smooth and of a kid glove texture; flavor strongly aromatic, with a suggestion of pineapple; pulp of fine texture with but few segments; almost entirely free from rag; a good keeper and shipper; its earliness (January to May) gives it commercial rank; medium size.

Tree. A good grower; thornless; leaves lanceolate, much more so than the general run of orange trees, and only slightly serrated and dark green in color; new wood inclined to grow slender but of good strength; general habit and appearance of tree strikingly individual.

History. This is another "sport" discovered in our growing orchards. Owing to the handsome and variegated exterior, often showing a narrow ridge of Washington Navel peel, combined with its fine eating qualities, induced us to propagate it and give it place in our published list of desirable varieties.

VANILLA ORANGE

Fruit. Medium size, round; skin smooth. Flesh quite juicy and with a distinct vanilla flavor when fully ripe.

Tree. A strong upright grower and quite prolific.

History. Introduced from Florida.

BITTER SEVILLE

Fruit. Round, medium to small, quite bitter. Used almost exclusively for making marmalades.

Tree. Fairly vigorous and quite prolific.

History. Probably brought originally from Spain to Florida and later introduced into California.

SWEET SEVILLE

Fruit. In size from small to medium; flavor delightfully sweet and pleasant; peel thin and smooth; color a strong yellow. Season February to March.

Tree. A good grower, prolific, and bears when quite young.

History. Another introduction from Florida.

Golden Buckeye Navel orange

ORNAMENTAL VARIETIES OF ORANGES

BOUQUET DES FLEURS

Fruit. Medium size; peel like that of a King orange; color orange yellow; a fine marmalade is made of the fruit by slicing as a whole; also the Bergamot oil of commerce.

Tree. Distinct in appearance, owing to the peculiar shape of its leaves, which are round, thick, leathery, compactly and densely furnished; flowers large and in clusters; free bloomer.

History. An introduction from the south of Europe; worthy of recognition on account of its oddity as well as economic values.

GOLDEN VARIEGATED

Fruit. In general characteristics very much like the Pomelo.

Tree. An ornamental acquisition with leaves of the same shape and design as the ordinary orange with the exception that they are beautifully marked with yellow configurations.

History. Brought from Europe by the late John Rock, of the California Nursery Company, and by it disseminated.

VARIEGATED NAVEL

Fruit. Similar to other navels excepting that the peel is marked with silver configurations the same as the foliage; quality rather inferior to other navels.

Tree. Inclined to be of slow growth and a lighter green foliage, the leaves having silver markings or configurations. When kept properly pruned makes a very ornamental tree.

History. A sport or bud mutation from the Washington Navel and propagated for its ornamental value.

STANDARD VARIETIES—KID GLOVE ORANGES

DANCY TANGERINE

Fruit. Of medium size; color bright shiny orange red; peel smooth, thin and leathery, being easily removed; flesh dark orange color, rather coarse grained; juice abundant and somewhat colored; flesh melting and free from "rag"; flavor pungent and sprightly; seeds from 6 to 18. Season February to May.

Tree. Strong upright grower, resembling in habit a seedling orange; when bearing heavily has a slight tendency to spread at top, which can be avoided by proper pruning; unlike most of its family, has a broad leaf, much like the standard oranges; well grown, the tree makes a handsome appearance with its intensely colored fruits; to enhance size and quality of fruit, it should be thinned out.

History. It is generally supposed that Dancy is a seedling from China. In this country the variety was undoubtedly disseminated in Florida from whence it found its way to California. It was known as early as 1843. Cuttings of trees propagated from this original planting strongly resemble the Dancy as we know it today.

KING MANDARIN

Fruit. Very large and flattened with loosely adhering peel and segments; color bright orange red; peel rough but of good appearance; pulp melting and free from rag; flavor peculiarly aromatic and agreeable; seeds 15 to 20 in number; general qualities of the very best. Season June to August.

Tree. Rather rigid and upright in growth; foliage a rich dark green color; generally quite thorny.

History. Introduced into California from Cochin China in 1882 by Dr. R. Magee of Riverside.

Spray of Dancy Tangerine oranges

WILLOW LEAVED MANDARIN

Fruit. Medium size, flattened; deep yellow; skin thin; segments loosely adherent; flesh dark orange-yellow, spicy and aromatic. Highly esteemed for eating out of hand because peel separates readily from the pulp; rated as one of the best of the kid glove type.

Tree. A compact grower, forming a beautiful umbrageous head, hence exceedingly desirable as an ornamental feature of the orchard or garden.

History. Introduced from Italy into Louisiana in about 1845, from which state it has been disseminated throughout Florida and California.

SATSUMA: OONSHIU, KII SEEDLESS

Fruit. Medium, flattened; the color is not red, like the Dancy Tangerine, but a deeper yellow than the Mandarin; rind and segments partly free; flesh fine grained, tender, sweet, juicy and delicious; entirely seedless. Season November to April.

Tree. Thornless and of spreading dwarf habit; leaves narrow; branches reclinate; a slow grower and bears young.

History. The Satsuma is a Japanese sort, and is said to have been first introduced into Florida in 1876 by Dr. Geo. R. Hall, and later (1878) by Mrs. Van Valkenburg. It first attracted attention in California in the eighties.

KUMQUATS (Variety Nagami)

Fruit. About an inch long and olive or egg-shaped; color a rich golden yellow; peel (which is edible) smooth, aromatic and spicy to the taste; juice somewhat sparse but acidulous; sections usually five; seeds two to five. The whole fruit, rind and all, is eaten and people become very fond of it. Preserved in sugar or crystallized the Kumquat, wherever it is known, is deservedly popular.

A Kumquat tree ready for planting

Tree. Dwarf and bushy in habit; usually when full grown 8 to 12 feet in diameter; forming a shapely head, rendering it an ornament as a tub plant or placed in the garden. An enormous bearer, which retains its fruit for months, giving it an added appearance of beauty as well as utility.

History. Downing in his Horticulturist for February, 1850, makes mention of the Kumquat as a greenhouse plant. At a later period it undoubtedly found its way into Florida. Reasoner Brothers imported the egg-shaped variety in 1885 and the round (known as Nagami) in 1890. During the rapid development of our citrus industry from about 1875 to 1895, this fruit undoubtedly found its way, with many others, to California from Florida.

ALGERIAN TANGERINE

Fruit. Similar in appearance to the Dancy Tangerine but matures much earlier. Of excellent quality and size; nearly seedless.

Oonshiu or Satsuma orange

Tree. A vigorous upright grower and fully as prolific as the Dancy. We consider it a valuable introduction.

History. Introduced by Geo. C. Roeding from buds sent from Algiers by Dr. Trabut of the French Government Experiment Station.

Willow-leaved Mandarin orange

ALGERIAN MANDARIN

Fruit. Similar in appearance to the ordinary Mandarin but ripens very much earlier. The quality is good.

Tree. Not quite as vigorous as other types of Mandarins, but is very productive and its fine willow like foliage makes it a very attractive tree for home and ornamental planting.

King Mandarin orange

History. Introduced by Geo. C. Roeding from buds sent here by Dr. Trabut at the same time the Algerian Tangerine buds were sent.

STANDARD VARIETIES OF LEMONS

EUREKA LEMON

Fruit. In shape oblong and of medium size; peel of fine texture and good protective quality and rich yellow color; flavor of strong citrus quality; juice free and abundant, with but little "rag"; cures and keeps well, giving it high rank in the trade.

Tree. Stalwart grower and comparatively free from thorns; prolific bearer, blooming and setting fruit continuously throughout the year, but especially a good cropper during the summer months.

History. Originated as a chance seedling in the grounds of Mr. C. R. Workman, from seed imported in 1872 from Hamburg. A few years later its fine qualities attracted Mr. Thomas A. Garey, one of the leading nurserymen of that day, who commenced to propagate large numbers of trees of this variety by budding, thus exploiting and pioneering the way to its dissemination pretty much over California, wherever the lemon finds congenial conditions.

Lisbon lemon

Eureka lemon

LISBON LEMON

Fruit. Of recognized merit in the markets of the country; fruit of average size; peel smooth, sweet to the taste, pure lemon color, and of medium thickness; flesh fine grained, nearly transparent and abundant juice; flavor strongly acidulous and free from bitterness; practically seedless; keeping and shipping qualities of the best.

Tree. Of largest growth; thorny; strong vigorous grower well covered with foliage and a good bearer of fruit, running uniform in size and even maturity.

History. The Lisbon is an importation from Portugal, and found its early exploitation and development in Riverside, where it was first made known by D. N. Burnham. In the earlier period of our citrus development it occupied the place of honor, but its position has been superseded by the Eureka.

VILLA FRANCA LEMON

Fruit. Size medium to large and oblong in form; peel smooth, of good texture and bright yellow in color with no trace of bitterness; flesh fine grained and translucent; juice abundant with little pulp; a high grade commercial fruit.

Tree. Upright grower; practically thornless; branches spreading if not properly pruned; foliage abundant; a thrifty grower and good bearer, setting its fruit well into the protection of its own foliage.

History. The Villa Franca was introduced into this country by General Sanford, and first planted in Florida, where it soon made a place for itself. In the late eighties it was brought from Florida to California. In the former state it occupies first place as a commercial lemon.

NEW AND RARE VARIETIES OF LEMONS

SWEET LEMON

Fruit. Small in size and rather flattened; color grayish yellow; flesh a dark lemon color; juice sweet and insipid with slight lemon flavor.

Tree. A vigorous grower but of spreading habit. Only worthy of propagation as a curiosity.

History. A Florida introduction.

DWARF LEMON (Citrus Limonium)

Fruit. Somewhat smaller than other lemons, but of about the same shape and quality.

Tree. More of a bush than a tree. Never attains very large size and is suitable for planting where space is limited. Very prolific.

History. Said to have originally come from China.

CEDROLA

Fruit. A species of citron but in appearance and flavor resembles a lemon. Used in connection with certain religious ceremonies. Quality of fruit good but quite seedy.

Tree. Rather of dwarf habits but very prolific.

History. A species of Citrus medica, indegenous to southern Asia, from whence it found its way to the Mediterranean and later to this continent.

PONDEROSA LEMON

Fruit. Very large, rough and coarse, but full of juice, of excellent quality. A desirable variety for home use but of no commercial value.

Tree. Inclined to be of dwarf habit and quite thorny. Very prolific, having bloom and fruit of all sizes the year around.

History. A Florida introduction.

ORNAMENTAL LEMONS

VARIEGATED LEMON

Fruit. Average in size, mottled and streaked; juice good quality; color variegated; flesh somewhat pink in color.

Tree. Strikingly individual from the fact that its shining, lustrous foliage is beautifully veined and marked with strong yellow-colored configurations, which give it a royal and handsome appearance as a specimen plant in the garden or on the lawn.

History. Originated some years ago as a sport, and propagated in a small way solely for its ornamental values, which give it high rank in landscape effects.

Growers should not fail to add a few trees of the little known varieties of citrus fruits for the home garden. Many of these possess an ornamental value that adds much to the beauty of home grounds. Among the more desirable ones we suggest a tree or two of Algerian Tangerine and Mandarin, Sampson Tangelo and Citrus limonium.

STANDARD LIMES

MEXICAN LIME

Fruit. Rather small in size, oblong or oval; color a pale lemon yellow; peel smooth and thin; flesh fine grained and grayish-green in color; juice abundant and translucent; acid strong; flavor decidedly that of the lime rather than lemon; almost seedless.

Tree. Medium and compact, growing from 10 to 25 feet in height; thorny; often cultivated as a hedge plant.

History. This variety was beyond question first introduced at an early period into Old Mexico by the Spaniards, from whence it found its way to California and Florida.

TAHITI LIME (Bearss Seedless)

Fruit. Size of a small lemon, decidedly oval in shape; peel smooth and thin; flesh fine grained with a greenish tinge; juice plentiful and practically colorless; acid pure and strong; flavor of the best; seedless; also known as Bearss Seedless.

Tree. Of good shape, 10 to 25 feet high, with a good spread of limbs; fruit produced singly and in clusters, well protected by foliage; slightly thorny.

History. An introduction from the Island of Tahiti.

NEW AND RARE VARIETIES OF LIMES

RANGPUR LIME (Red Lime)

Fruit. Both the peel and pulp have a rich reddish color. The peel is loose, somewhat like the Mandarin. The juice has the acidity of the Lime and Lemon.

Tree. Fairly vigorous growth and said to be as hardy as the Lemon.

History. Introduced from India.

THORNLESS LIME

Fruit. Medium size and good quality, having the true lime flavor.

Tree. Compact and uniform in growth and practically thornless. Quite ornamental in appearance.

History. Introduced from South America by Dr. Franceschi of Santa Barbara.

SWEET LIME

Fruit. Of medium size with an abundance of highly flavored juice and unlike other limes it contains less acid and more sugar, making it quite sweet to the taste.

Tree. Fairly vigorous but quite tender. Should be planted in a warm location.

History. Introduced by the U. S. Department of Agriculture from Europe.

STANDARD POMELOS

MARSH'S SEEDLESS POMELO

Fruit. Medium size; peel thin, with half the usual bitter; a true pomelo (grape fruit) and not a hybrid; practically seedless, specimens with merely rudimentary seeds being rare; juice abundant and of exceptionally fine flavor; flesh dark and rich. . In serving you are not required to remove from 25 to 40 seeds, as is necessary with the common grape fruit, but is ready for the table when cut in halves; being devoid of seeds to germinate when left late on the trees or in storage, enhances its keeping qualities, which is a great factor in its favor; cures and keeps like the lemon.

Tree. Strong, vigorous, compact, grower, and when at its best is indeed an object of beauty with its liberal furnishing of rich deep green foliage and great bunches of pure lemon-yellow globe-shaped fruit; a good bearer; quality and flavor of fruit is greatly enhanced by liberal dressings of fertilizer to the soil; when setting a heavy crop, the fruit should be thinned out, thus affording the tree opportunity to perfect the remaining fruits, insuring quality, size and volume of juice.

History. The Marsh Seedless Pomelo was originally introduced by Mr. C. M. Marsh, of Lakeland, Florida, in 1895-96. The original tree was a seedling, and the fruit being without seed and of good flavor, at once brought it into public notice. Its introduction into California occurred about twenty years ago. The Shaddock, to which the Pomelo belongs, is native to the Malayan and Polynesian Islands.

TRIUMPH

Fruit. Medium; peel smooth, clear, thin and fine-grained; less "rag" than in most grapefruits, and fewer seeds; very heavy; juicy and well flavored. There is no bitter in the juice, flesh or membrane surrounding the cells and dividing the segments, and very little in the white inner lining of the peel. Like the preceding, the fruit cures and keeps equally as well as the lemon.

Tree. Of good habit and comes into bearing young; prolific. Among the best of the later introductions.

Marsh Seedles pomelo

History. The original Triumph Pomelo is said to have been a chance seedling discovered in the grounds of the Orange Grove Hotel at Tampa, Florida. Its commercial dissemination dates from about the year 1885; some years later it found its way to Southern California, and soon attained rank with shippers as well as growers.

DUNCAN POMELO

Fruit. In shape it is slightly oblate and of desirable size for commercial use, color clear yellow, with oil cells showing through the skin; very juicy and said to contain more of the true grapefruit flavor than any other fruit. In Florida it ripens in December but can be left on the tree until May without deterioration. One of the leading varieties in Florida.

Tree. Quite vigorous and very hardy, said to withstand a temperature that will seriously damage other varieties. The original Duncan tree is still producing good crops of fruit although more than 80 years old.

History. Introduced by the Glen Saint Mary Nurseries from a seedling in the grove of A. L. Duncan, Duneda, Florida.

IMPERIAL

Fruit. Very similar to the Marsh Seedless in size, shape and color; peel smooth and fine grained; juice abundant; little rag; flavor sweet and pleasant; good keeper; seeds more or less pronounced.

Tree. A strong upright compact grower; fruit well distributed throughout the bearing surface; fruits from second to third year after tree has been planted in orchard form; habit good, making a fine symmetrical appearance, true to the pomelo type.

History. A chance Florida introduction, given the name Imperial, in California.

FOSTER POMELO

Fruit. Large in size, running from 48s to 64s, which are the most desirable sizes commercially. Peel smooth and fairly thin; flesh purplish pink next to the skin changing to a clear translucent color at the center, has the true pomelo flavor with very little rag; one of the earliest varieties to ripen.

Tree. Of vigorous upright growth.

History. Said to be a sport of the well-known Walters variety grown in Florida.

ODD CITRUS VARIETIES

SAMPSON TANGELO

Fruit. Compresseed spherical, slightly drawn out at stem end like tangerine; of medium size, color chrome yellow, considerably darker than the pomelo, though not so red as the tangerine; skin thin, about one-eighth of an inch in thickness, loose and easily removed, surface smooth and glossy; segments 9 to 11, separating easily like tangerine; membranes thin and tender; rag very slight; quality excellent; texture very tender and juicy; flavor slightly sub-acid, somewhat sweeter than pomelo, medium in size.

Tree. A vigorous, strong, upright grower, and in the opinion of its originators will prove productive; no hardier than either of its parents, the Dancy Tangerine and ordinary Pomelo, foliage more like the latter than the former.

History. The hybrid seedling from which this variety was developed was grown and fruited by Mr. F. G. Sampson, of Boardman, Florida. On the suggestion of the Department of Agriculture at Washington, we have adopted the name of "Sampson Tangelo."

BUN-TAN

Fruit. About the size of a large pomelo with rather thick skin, light yellow in color. Flesh quite like a pomelo but with a pink tinge; has a distinct but quite agreeable flavor.

Tree. Vigorous and in appearance quite like the Pomelo.

History. Said to be of Japanese origin.

CITRANGE

Fruit. Entirely different in flavor from any other citrus fruit and said to make a very desirable drink, taking the place of orange or lemonade.

Tree. Very hardy and quite vigorous. The value of this variety lies in its hardiness and ability to grow where the temperature goes too low to grow any other citrus fruits. Can be grown in the Southern Gulf Coast States, also in Northern California and parts of Oregon.

History. An introduction by the Department of Agriculture, being a cross between the common sweet orange and Citrus Trifoliata.

THE CITRON OF COMMERCE

Fruit. Oblong, and conical in shape; skin thick, warty and furrowed in some varieties, while smooth in others; color lemon-yellow and highly scented; pulp less acid than the lemon. The Citron of Commerce is manufactured from this fruit, and it also yields an essential oil. The amount of citron rind sold in the United States amounts to 12,000 cases of 250 pounds each, every ounce of which is imported. Its manufacture in California has been demonstrated.

Tree. Rather dwarf in habit, and inclined to sprawl, but with its large light green foliage makes a very presentable appearance; it is somewhat susceptible to frost; fruits and blossoms throughout the year.

History. Introduced into California both by private enterprise and on the initiative of the Department of Agriculture at Washington.

CITRUS TREES FOR THE HOME GROUNDS

No one thing has done more to increase the production of California citrus orchards than bud selection. All the care and labor expended on unproductive or inferior fruiting trees will not make them produce good fruit, and all such trees should be rebudded to productive strains selected from record bearing trees. In buying trees from nurserymen using nothing but selected buds the danger of having unproductive trees or an inferior quality of fruit is eliminated. The same labor and care expended on selected trees will produce remunerative returns, whereas only loss and disappointmnt is the result if unproven stock is planted.

A busy scene in the San Dimas orange packing house.

HANDLING THE CROP

IN the earlier days of California citrus culture it was not uncommon to find a small packing plant at most every orchard of any size, but such is not the case now. Only the larger growers, having sufficient acreage to warrant a good sized house, have their individual plants. With the numerous packing houses in almost every locality operated either by private packers or local association of growers, it is no longer necessary for the grower of 5, 10, or 20 acres of fruit to have a private plant, in fact these packing concerns have picking crews, working under the supervision of competent foremen, that come to the orchard and pick the fruit and if necessary, convey it to the packing house. The particular advantage of this is that these picking crews are experienced men, knowing how to properly pick and handle the fruit so that it will reach the packing house in the best possible condition.

Upon the proper handling of the fruit largely depends its carrying quality, and careless picking and handling often causes heavy losses in decayed fruit before it reaches the market. A slight cut with the orange clippers, scratch with the finger nails or bruise from dropping the fruit in the boxes will start decay and one such fruit placed in a box often times causes the loss of the entire box of fruit. It therefore behooves the grower, whether he picks his own fruit or hires it done, to use every care in seeing that it is properly handled from the trees to the packing house. The picking should be done with the latest improved clippers. These clippers are so constructed that they will not bruise the fruit. The stems should be cut as closely as possible so as not to leave a long stem on the fruit to bruise other fruit in the box. Never allow either oranges or lemons to be pulled from the tree as it invariably spoils them for shipping and they will be thrown out as culls. Use a regular picking sack made of canvas with the bottom so arranged that it can be opened and the fruit let out in that way rather than being poured out from the top. This allows the picker to empty his sack into the boxes without bruising the fruit. The field boxes are usually supplied by the packing house handling the crop. Never fill them more than level full so that in stacking, the boxes will not smash or bruise the top fruit. In hauling to the packing house use a wagon or conveyance with good springs. Many houses will not accept fruit hauled on a wagon without springs. With the more general use of the auto truck for this work, horse drawn vehicles are being displaced and for hauling any distance they are not only much faster but much easier on the fruit.

The modern packing house equipment is so designed that all unnecessary handling is eliminated and from the time the fruit is received at the door until it

Twenty carloads of boxes of oranges direct from the pickers ready for grading and packing.

is loaded in the cars for shipment every known device is used to prevent bumps and bruises. As the field boxes are taken from the wagon or truck they are usually set on belt or roller conveyors which carry them to the storage room. From here it is trucked to the elevator which carries the boxes, and automatically dumps the fruit into a hopper from which it passes through the brusher, which cleans it of all dust and dirt as it passes through. From here it passes on to the sorting table where the necessary help inspects each orange and sorts out the different grades, placing each on separate conveyors which carry the fruit to the grader or sizer running that particular grade of fruit.

The common grades are designated as Fancy, Choice, Standards and culls, although some houses run additional grades known as Extra Fancy and Extra Choice. Only such oranges as are perfect in shape, color, texture and without blemishes are run in the Fancy or Extra Fancy grades. The choice or Extra Choice grade consists of all first class fruit not quite up to the standard necessary for the first grade. That is, they may not be quite so highly colored, of just a little rougher texture or may have some small blemishes, but nothing that will tend to affect their keeping or carrying quality. The standard grade consists of such fruit as will not pass for Fancy or Choice but that is sound and of marketable quality. All fruit that shows sign of having been bruised in handling or where the peel is checked or split so as to impair its keeping quality and all rough inferior fruits are put into the culls. In former years these were sorted over, the poorer ones being dumped and the best of them sold to peddlers at a few cents a box and came more or less in competition with the better grade of fruit. With the establishment of Citrus By-Product factories, most of these culls are now used up in the manufacture of marmalades, jellies, extracts, etc., and while the price obtained for such fruit is not great it tends to prevent it from being placed on the market to break down the price of good fruit.

The modern packing houses are equipped with separate graders for each grade of fruit run, also with automatic scales so that as the fruit passes from the sorting tables each grade is weighed before passing onto the grader and the grower knows just how many pounds of each grade has been run for him. Where automatic scales are not used, it is necessary to keep each grower's fruit separate until it is packed, making what is known as a "clean up" after each run, so as to ascertain the number of boxes of the different grades the grower's fruit packed out.

As the fruit passes onto the graders, which consists of a series of revolving rollers set for the different sizes to be packed, the smaller fruit drops out first and the larger sizes pass on to the end, being the last to drop out. As the fruit drops through, it passes to packing bins arranged for each size. The packers take the fruit from these bins and after wrap-

STANDARD PACKS FOR ORANGES USED BY THE TRADE IN CALIFORNIA

192 PACK TANGERINES

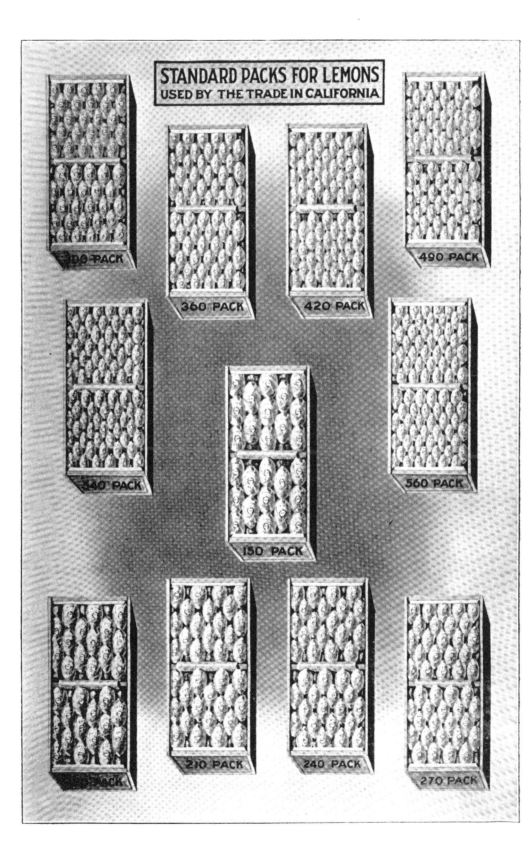

ping it in tissue wrapping paper, cut for the different sizes, it is packed in the boxes for shipment. All fruit is packed by a regular standard, and each size has a certain definite way in which the fruit must be placed in the box. The standard orange box is divided into two compartments, each being 11½x11½x11½ inches, inside measurement and the standard grades are 64s, 80s, 100s, 126s, 150s, 176s, 200s, 216s, 250s, and 324s. In grading the fruit it is always run just a little large so that when packed, it will fit tightly in the boxes and when the last layer is placed, it should be about two inches above the top of the box. This allows for any shrinkage that may occur in transit and prevents the possibility of the fruit becoming loose and shaking around in the box. As the packers complete the packing operation, the boxes are placed on another conveyer which carries them to the press where the lids and center strips are nailed on and the fruit is ready to be loaded in the cars.

For local shipments ordinary box cars are used, but for Northern and Eastern markets the regular ventilated refrigerator cars are the only ones that it is safe to ship in. For winter shipments these cars are usually closed tight or ventilated, according to weather conditions in the section through which they are passing, but all summer shipments are sent out under ice to prevent decay. Formerly the standard car of oranges contained 362 to 384 packed boxes, but the shortage of refrigerator cars has made it necessary to load heavier and under government control the railway officials insisted on what is known as a solid load whch required 462 boxes, and with the return to pre-war conditions the railroads are still insisting on the heavier loads. During the present season the California Fruit Growers' Exchange has been experimenting with water transportaton with very satisfactory results, which would indicate that a large part of the citrus fruit for eastern and middle west consumption will in the future be shipped by water as the fruit not only carries with very little decay, but at a considerable saving in freight charges.

The process of handling lemons is somewhat different from that of handling oranges. In picking lemons they are taken according to size rather than degree of ripeness and it is customary for the pickers to use a ring of the proper size to prevent picking under size fruit. For winter picking 2 5-16 inch rings are used and for spring and summer picking 2 1-2 inch rings.

Lemons are picked every month or six weeks throughout the year. Those picked during the winter months are put in storage and held for the spring and summer trade, while those picked later are only held in the curing rooms long enough to allow them to properly color and become somewhat pliable so as to facilitate packing.

Up to the present time no grader has been manufactured that will successfully grade lemons and therefore this work must all be done by hand. The grades as to quality are the same as with oranges but the pack is entirely different, the standard lemon box being 10½ x 14 x 27 inches outside measurements, divided into two compartments, and the packs are 210s, 240s, 270s, 300s, 360s, 420s, and 490s. These figures represent the number of lemons of the different sizes there are in a box.

Pomelos are also graded by hand but are packed in the standard orange box, the sizes being 36s, 48s, 64s, 80s and 96s.

The 36's, 48's and 64's are the sizes most in demand, and as pomelos are very prolific it is sometime adviable to thin the fruit when it is small in order to give that remaining a chance to attain marketable size.

Standard pomelo packs.

A standard lemon pack.

Standard orange packs.

A standard Tangerine pack.

The above illustrations convey a clear idea of the standard commercial packs of citrus fruits as they appear when opened and placed on sale at points of destination. The ends of the boxes are invariably embellished with a beautiful colored label, while the sides are stenciled with the name of the shipper. Note the regular manner in which the fruit "opens up," which has much to do with its appearance and selling qualities.

Bearing habit of the better strains of avocado trees

TROPICAL FRUITS IN CALIFORNIA

AVOCADOS

AUTHORITIES tell us that the native home of the Avocado is Southern Mexico. From there it was introduced into the tropical sections of Central and South America. In 1526 Gonzalo Hernandez de Oviedo gave the first written account of the Avocado, having seen trees growing in Columbia near the Isthmus of Panama. Other explorers report its presence in Mexico and Central America during the sixteenth century, referring to it as an article of food amongst the natives. In these tropical countries it takes the place of meat to a very large extent. The natives of Guatemala consider a few tortillas, an Avocado and a cup of coffee a very good meal.

The Avocado contains a higher percentage of oil and fat, some varieties going as high as 30%. The protein content is also higher than in any other fresh fruit.

It will be seen from this that it ranks high as a food and its consumption will be much more general amongst the people of the United States as they become acquainted with its true food value.

There are three different groups of Avocados: the West Indian, Guatemalan and Mexican.

The distinction is, however, less between the West Indian and the Guatemalan, the principal difference being in the hardiness of the tree and the thickness of the peel of the fruit, the former being more susceptible to cold and the peel thinner and more of a leathery texture. The foliage is also of a lighter shade than in the Guatemalan type.

Up to the present time practically all of the commercial plantings in Florida have been of the West Indian varieties, but in California they have not proven successful on account of their inability to withstand our winter climate.

The Guatemalan type being a native of the highlands of Guatemala, where the climate corresponds more nearly to that of California, seem to be better adapted to our conditions and the few old seedling trees now growing in different sections indicate that this type will thrive wherever oranges or lemons are not damaged by cold weather.

The Mexican type is the most hardy of any of the Avocados, but the fruit (with a few exceptions) has a very thin skin and is much smaller than either the West Indian or Guatemalan. The seed in most all fruits of this type is inclined to be loose in the cavity. This, together with the thin skin, makes them undesirable for shipping.

EARLY INTRODUCTION INTO CALIFORNIA

As far as known the first introduction of Avocados into California was made in 1871 by R. B. Ord, who brought three trees from Mexico and planted them at Santa Barbara. Other trees and seeds were brought in and planted from time to time after that date. The Miller, Murrietta and Chappelow trees were some of the earliest. Many of the earlier plantings were killed by frosts on account of being either planted in localities not suited to their culture, or being varieties of the more tender sorts not adapted to our climatic conditions. Only after it was seen that the more hardy Mexican varieties would survive and produce fruit here was any effort made to propagate the better and larger sorts.

The Fuerte avocado tree: one of the leading varieties for commercial planting

About 1910 sufficient interest was created, by the fruiting of some of the Guatemalan seedlings then growing in different sections of Southern California, so that explorations were made into the highlands of Mexico and Guatemala in search of better and more frost resistant sorts, as a result of which we now have a number of desirable varieties that give promise of placing the industry on a substantial commercial basis in this state.

In May, 1915, a number of people interested in Avocado culture in California formed an organization known as the California Avocado Association, the object being to work together in establishing the Avocado culture on a more substantial basis. Due

The Sharpless avocado; in habit tree a tall grower and good producer.

to the efforts of these pioneers great advancement has been made in the introduction and selection of new and valuable varieties, as well as in the elimination of those that have no commercial value, also in cultural practices and in handling and marketing the fruit. At the present time the Association has over four hundred members and the attendance at their semi-annual meetings shows the interest manifested in Avocado growing. A close study has been made of the varieties now bearing, and only those that have real commercial merit are recommended to planters.

A bud selection department has also been organized and individual tree records are being kept so that nurserymen and orchardists may secure buds of known parentage, thus assuring the planter trees that will prove to be prolific and true to name.

seed is started in beds and when sufficiently matured transplanted to the field (much the same manner as citrus seedlings), and when large enough are budded

A symmetrical Dickinson avocado tree; a vigorous grower and good producer.

We would earnestly recommend that all parties interested in Avocado culture join this Association, as their annual and semi-annual reports (issued in book form) are alone worth the nominal membership fee.

GROWING AND TRANSPLANTING THE NURSERY TREES

For the purposes of insuring increased hardiness the Mexican seedlings are used as root stocks. The

to the varieties desired. Much care is necessary, however, in budding, and both seedlings and buds must be in proper condition to make the operation successful. After the buds start to grow the seedling tops are cut off and the young buds trained to stakes the same as with citrus stock.

In taking up Avocados it is advisable to ball them, although under certain conditions they may be moved "open roots", but this method is very hazardous at best, hence we do not advise it only where impossible to take them out with balls of earth.

Before starting to transplant them all new or ten-

A fine specimen Spinks avocado tree; yielding fruit weighing from 28 to 30 ounces.

der growth should be pruned off, care being taken to paint all large cuts. This should be done several days before the trees are dug. As with citrus trees, it is advisable to place the trees in a lath house, or under partial shade for a few days after digging, before planting in orchard form. This gives the trees a chance to recover from the shock of digging; under more favorable conditions they will start to grow more quickly and generally grow better than when moved direct from the nursery to the orchard.

After planting it is best to shade the trees until more readily. This can be done by driving four stakes and spreading burlap over the top and on the south side; the idea being to protect the trees from the direct rays of the sun from about 10 a. m. to 4 p. m.

As Avocados are susceptible to sunburn it is important that the trunks be protected until the trees have sufficient top to shade themselves.

CLIMATE AND SOIL

It is safe to say that Avocados of the Guatemalan type will do well wherever lemons are successfully grown, while those of the Mexican type will withstand any temperature that does not damage oranges. This of course applies to bearing trees. Young trees just out of the nursery will not stand as low a temperature as those that have reached maturity, and therefore need some protection for the first two or three winters, especially if planted where the temperature is apt to go below 32 degrees F.

Mexican seedling avocado trees in nursery rows

Another climatic condition that must be taken into consideration in the successful growing of Avocados is humidity. The Avocado being a native of the tropics naturally prefers a humid atmosphere and therefore is at its best when grown within a reasonable distance from the coast. Trees planted in the hot interior valleys do not do as well as those enjoying coastal conditions, due to the dryness of the atmosphere rather than to the heat; it has been observed that trees planted in such localities shed their leaves in the heat of summer, no matter how moist the soil is kept. It will therefore be seen that the best locations for Avocado culture, from a climatic standpoint, are to be found in the warmer sections between the coast and the first mountain range.

Another climatic condition to be taken into consideration is the danger from heavy winds

In regard to soil the Avocado does not seem to be over particular, hence they will grow on almost any kind of soil, provided it is of sufficient depth and the drainage good. Trees do best, however, when planted in a deep loamy soil. They should not be planted where the water level is within three feet of the surface. As we depend entirely on irrigation during the summer months it is not essential that the water level be at any set distance, just so it does not come to within three feet of the surface.

PLANTING SEASON

The best time to plant Avocados is from March 1 to April 30, but they may be planted at any time during the summer provided proper care is exercised. It is not advisable to plant during the winter months on account of the danger of frosts. It is best to plant as early after March 1 as possible, as the trees then become established while the weather is moderate and they are in better condition to stand the summer heat. They will also have the advantage of a longer growing season, and thus be in a hardier condition for their first winter in the orchard.

DISTANCE TO PLANT

The slower growing varieties, and also those that make more of an upright growth, may be planted from 20 to 25 feet each way, but the more thrifty trees and those of a spreading habit should be planted not closer than 30 feet apart. This also depends somewhat on the nature of the soil, as trees planted in a heavy rich soil make a more vigorous growth than on the lighter soils. If uncertain as to the proper distance to plant, give the trees the benefit of the doubt by planting them a little further apart. It is better to give them too much room rather than have them crowded when they come into full bearing.

Standard sizes of balled avocado trees
2 to 3 feet, 3 to 4, 4 to 5, and 5 to 8.

PLANTING

Planting is much the same as with citrus trees. On heavy soils, where the drainage is not apt to be good, it is best to blast the holes before planting, but the trees must not be planted until the earth has been thoroughly settled again with water. Set the trees as near as possible the same depth as they grew in the nursery, and never more than one or two inches above the top of the ball. Fill the holes with surface soil and water immediately. Do not mix fer-

A prolific Puebla avocado tree, habit erect with spreading branches.

tilizer of any kind with the soil used in filling the holes and it is best not to apply any fertilizer until after the trees have become established and started to make some growth. Unless the soil is very poor, do not fertilize until trees start to bear and at first use it very sparingly.

Budded Avocados are quite tender and easily damaged, so care must be exercised in handling. Never lift them by the trunk but always take hold of the ball from underneath or by the loose ends of the burlap above where it is tied in balling. Extreme care must be exercised in handling balled trees so as not to crack or break the ball in any way, or the benefit to be derived from balling is lost and the tree is apt to die.

As stated elsewhere, the Avocado is very susceptible to sunburn, so do not neglect to properly shade the tree as soon as planted. This covering should be

A well-developed fruiting avocado orchard.

left on for a month or more or until they have made some new growth. After this covering is removed tree protectors or some other covering should be put on the trunks and any exposed limbs should be either whitewashed or covered until sufficient top has been made to protect them from the direct rays of the sun.

CULTURAL DIRECTIONS

We are told that in the Tropics very little care is given Avocados, in fact, most of the trees grow in a comparative wild state; however, we must not assume that they will do well here under similar neglect, as our climatic conditions vary greatly from those of the Tropics, and therefore we must adopt methods more in accordance with those used in general orchard culture. It has been our observation that the Avocado orchards, where cultivation is practiced and the soil kept free from weeds or other vegetable growth, show better growth than where they are allowed to grow more as they do in the country of their nativity.

The Avocado is a vigorous growing tree, and therefore requires an abundance of moisture. Excepting in very heavy soils, where the drainage is inclined to be poor, it is almost impossible to give them too much water. This does not mean, however, that irrigation should be continuous. On light soils an irrigation every two or three weeks during the warmest part of the summer will keep them in good condition provided, of course, the soil is kept well cultivated between irrigations. On the heavier clay soils they should only be irrigated every three or four weeks, depending on the weather.

As yet but few growers agree as to proper methods of applying water and cultivation, no doubt due to the varied condition of the Southern California soils. A method that might be ideal in one section may prove to be entirely wrong in another, and thus it is more or less up to the individual planter to study his local conditions and treat his trees accordingly.

In the lighter soils the basin system of irrigation works very satisfactorily. These basins are made so that no water will reach the trunk of the tree and large enough to give the entire root system a thorough irrigation. Usually the basin should be just a little larger than the top diameter of the tree. If straw is available the basin can be filled with it and this will act as a mulch, and it will not be necessary to hoe or cultivate around the trees after each irrigation. During the winter and after the irrigation season is over it will be advisable to cultivate in the basin and work the straw into the soil where it may be converted into humus and plant food for the tree the following season.

On the heavier clay soils we doubt the advisability of using the basin system of irrigation, and think the furrow system, similar to that used in citrus orchards, will prove more satisfactory. Ordinarily we have sufficient rain so that winter irrigation is not necessary, however, it occasionally happens that due to irregular or a lack of rain, the trees may require some irrigation during the winter months. This would apply more particularly to trees of bearing age and during or just after the blooming stage, as the tree must not be allowed to suffer from want of moisture during the critical period, or the fruit will not set.

FERTILIZATION

This is another matter on which all planters are not agreed, some maintaining that the tree should not be fertilized until it comes into bearing, and then only very sparingly, while others advocate the use of fertilizer from the time the trees are first planted. This difference of opinion we think is also due to the difference in soil conditions, and each advocate may be right in his particular locality. On the lighter soils a little fertilizer applied intelligently after the first year will no doubt be of much benefit to the tree, while on the heavier soils it might produce too vigorous a growth and, as maintained by

Avocado tree fruiting in nursery row

some, cause the tree to be later in coming into bearing. The experiments made to date with the different fertilizers seem to indicate that well rotted barnyard manure gives better results than the commercial fertilizers. If the latter is used, it should be as far as possible of animal rather than mineral origin.

Bearing branch of Dicky A. avocado tree.

PRUNING

Very little attention has been given to this phase of Avocado culture, and to date there has not been

Lyon avocado tree; an early and prolific bearer

sufficient experiments made to determine just the proper methods to pursue with the different varieties. It is safe to say, however, that enough pruning should be done to cause the young tree to form a well-balanced head and frame work so that in after years it will be capable of holding its maximum capacity of fruit. Most varieties of Avocados form a very symmetrical head and little pruning is required. However, a little pruning when young in the way of making a proper distribution of the main branches will be of immense benefit to the tree in later years. All cuts, whether large or small, should be made smooth and carefully painted or waxed over immediately to prevent fungus or decay.

TOP WORKING AVOCADO TREES.

Most of the earlier plantings of Avocados were from seedling trees and many of these have proven unprofitable, either on account of the poor quality of the fruit or the failure of the trees to bear fruit.

All such can be top-worked to profitable varieties at less expense and a new top grown in much shorter time than would be necessary to grow a new tree to bearing age.

The strong vigorous root system of the older tree causes the grafts to make a remarkable growth and in two or three years the new top will be almost as large as the original tree.

Top-worked avocado tree 18 months from budding.

Top working by grafting gives more satisfactory results than budding and if the instructions here given are followed out carefully there should be no difficulty in getting a good stand of grafts.

The selection of the scions is most important. They should be hard, well matured wood cut from what is known as "second growth," with plump well formed buds but not too far advanced. The scions should be from 3/8 to 5/8 inches in diameter, depending on the size of the limbs to be grafted. The months of February, March and April are the best for grafting the Avocado.

The limbs to be grafted should be selected with a view of forming a well balanced head, so that when the remainder of the top is cut away the grafts will make a shapely tree. Select three to four such limbs evenly distributed and saw them off from two to four feet from the main trunk, depending on the size of the tree. If the limbs are large it is best to first cut them off a foot or more beyond where the grafts are to be inserted to avoid splitting and then resaw them at the desired location. This last cut should be made squarely across and at right angles to the limb. Smooth the surface of the cut with a knife and with a cleaver placed across the middle, split the stump far enough down so that the pressure will not be too great on the grafts. After removing the cleaver insert a wedge, made of some hard wood, in the center of the split and drive it in so that the grafts can be inserted without bruising.

In selecting the scions or grafts use the smaller scions for small limbs and the larger ones for the large limbs. The length of the scion is not important excepting that there should be at least two or three good buds beyond where it is inserted in the limb. Cut the lower end so as to form a wedge of about one inch in length. Extreme care should be used in cutting the wedge so that the sides will be perfectly smooth and fit perfectly. Insert one scion on each side of the split in the stump, remove the hard wood wedge carefully so that the scions are slightly pinched but easily moveable and then adjust them so that the outer edge of the scion comes in contact with the cambium layer or inner bark of the stump. This is important in all grafting operations, unless such contact is made the scion can not unite. After the scions are carefully adjusted remove the wedge completely and wrap the stump with waxed cloth from the surface down as far as the split shows on the sides. With a paint brush apply a good coating of hot grafting wax to the surface of the stump and over the waxed cloth, being sure that all parts are covered so as to exclude the air. On large stumps where the split between the scions is quite wide it is advisable to fill it with paper or cloth before applying the wax to prevent it from running off, also between the outer edge of the scion and the waxed cloth there may be an opening due to the difference in the thickness of the bark on the scion and that of the stump and this should be carefully filled with wax. The end of the scion should be sealed with either wax or paint to prevent its drying out.

After the grafting is complete wrap newspaper around the stumps so that it will extend out over the scions and protect them from the sun but not so as to interfere with their growth. Wherever possible leave one or two limbs on each stump to keep up the flow of sap and also one or two of main limbs where it is not necessary to cut them all off for grafting. These limbs should be left until the grafts have made considerable growth. The trunk and all exposed limbs should be well whitewashed to prevent sunburn.

After the grafts start to grow they should be carefully watched and where necessary supported to prevent their being broken by the wind. On account of their rapid growth they are quite apt to make more top than the union can support the first year and as a result the graft breaks out of the stump if not supported. This can be overcome somewhat if the growth is kept topped back and each graft is made to properly branch and thicken up as it grows.

THE FIVE RECOMMENDED VARIETIES OF THE STATE ASSOCIATION

PUEBLA (Mexican)

Fruit. True Mexican type, skin quite thin and a beautiful dark glossy purple when ripe. It is the smallest of the recommended varieties, weighing from six to fourteen ounces with a medium-sized seed which fits tightly in the cavity. The flesh is yellow, smooth and of a rich flavor. The period of eight months from blossom to maturity of the fruit is the shortest of any of the recommended varieties. Ripens in December and January.

Tree. A compact grower, erect and very hardy. Has proven to be an early and heavy bearer. Considered one of the best types of Avocados.

History. Introduced as budwood in 1911 by West India Gardens from Atlisco, Puebla, Mexico, under No. 13. One of the two varieties selected from over a hundred that were introduced from that section.

The prolific bearing Lyon avocado

FUERTE (Guatemalan)

Fruit. Pear-shaped, dull green in color and matures at an exceptionally good time. Weight from ten to sixteen ounces and has a medium-sized seed. Samples of the fruit have analyzed as high as 30 percent fat or oil, being one of the highest yet tested. This, together with its other good qualities, gives it rank as one of the best. Ripens January to March inclusive.

Tree. Very vigorous but of spreading habit, appears to be a hybrid of the Mexican and Guatemalan types and has proven to be the most hardy on the list. It bears early and regularly.

History. Introduced as budwood in 1911 from Atlisco, Puebla, Mexico, under No. 15. This is the only other variety selected from the one hundred odd varieties introduced from the highlands of Mexico.

SPINKS (Guatemalan)

Fruit. Varies from nearly round to slightly pear shape and weighs from sixteen to twenty ounces. The seed averages large in proportion to the flesh, but fits tightly in the cavity. The flesh is cream-colored, smooth and of a rich pleasant flavor. When fully mature, the thick purplish-black skin gives the fruit a very attractive appearance and makes it a particular favorite on the market. It is considered equal to the finest flavored Guatemalan fruits. Ripens April to June inclusive.

Tree. An unusually strong upright grower and has proven to be hardy and quite prolific.

History. The variety is of local origin, having been selected from a number of seedlings grown on Mr. W. A. Spink's place at Duarte, California. True Guatemalan type.

DICKINSON (Guatemalan)

Fruit. Oval to obovate in form, weighing from 12 to 18 ounces. The skin is unusually thick, woody and quite rough. When ripe the purple glossy color gives it a very handsome appearance. The seed is medium in size and fits tightly in the cavity. The flesh is a pale greenish yellow, free from fibre and has a rich, agreeable flavor. Ripens from May to September.

Tree. A strong rapid grower and a regular and early bearer.

History. The original tree was grown from a seed planted in 1899 by Mrs. M. J. Dickinson, Los Angeles. Belongs to the Guatemalan type.

SHARPLESS (Guatemalan)

Fruit. Pear-shaped and weighs from sixteen to twenty ounces. The surface is slightly pitted or roughened and is a beautiful bronze or dark maroon color when ripe. The flesh is cream-colored, smooth, free from fibre and of a very rich pleasant flavor. The seed is small and completely fills the cavity. In direct contrast to the Puebla, the quickest to mature, the Sharpless requires eighteen months from blossom to maturity of fruit. Ripens from September to January.

Tree. A strong upright grower and trees budded from the parent tree indicate that it will be an early and regular bearer. The difficulty in propagating this variety makes it rather more expensive to raise and therefore it will probably always be higher priced than other varieties.

History. Introduced by B. H. Sharpless of Santa Ana, California, where the original tree is now growing.

The Dickinson and Sharpless are not considered quite as hardy as the first three varieties and should only be planted where lemons are considered safe from frost.

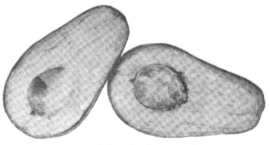

Fruit of the Sharpless avocado

If the orchardist or home grower will plant these five proven varieties, he will be assured of a succession of fruit during every month in the year. The bearing seasons given are the months during which the principal or main crop may be marketed. Many trees will mature a few fruits before this time and also hold fruits much later than the months specified, but such fruits usually represent a small percentage of the total yield.

VARIETIES OF MORE OR LESS COMMERCIAL IMPORTANCE

LYON (Guatemalan)

Fruit. Shape pyriform, weighs from sixteen to eighteen ounces. Skin moderately thick and somewhat rough; dark green in color with numerous small yellowish or russet dots. Flesh a deep cream tinged with green toward the skin and has a rich pleasant flavor. Seed of medium size, fitting tightly in the cavity. Ripens April to August.

Tree. Very upright in its growth but not so vigirous as some of the other varieties. It is an early and prolive bearer, often setting fruit while yet in the nursery row. On account of its tall, slender growth this variety can be planted much closer together than other sorts; fifteen feet apart each way being considered not too close by some growers.

History. Originated at Hollywood from seed imported by L. Lyon in 1913. Of Guatemalan origin.

BLAKEMAN (Guatemalan)

Fruit. Pyriform, weighing from sixteen to twenty ounces. Skin thick and woody, slightly roughened and dark green in color. Flesh a deep cream yellow tinged with green near the skin; flavor rich and pleasant; quality good. Seed medium size fitting rightly in the cavity. Ripens April to August.

Tree. A strong grower but its spreading tendency necessitates early pruning to produce a compact head; it is fairly hardy and a good bearer.

History. Originated at Hollywood from seed brought in by John Murrietta and planted in 1904. First described in the Journal of Agriculture for November, 1913, under the name of Dickey No. 2. It has also been known as Habersham.

TAFT (Guatemalan)

Fruit. Obvate to pyriform; weight sixteen ounces, skin thick and somewhat roughened, deep green in color. Flesh cream colored, smooth and of excellent flavor. Seed of medium size fitting tightly in the cavity. Ripens May to October.

Tree. A rapid grower of spreading habit. Not considered sufficiently hardy to plant where there is danger of heavy frosts. Also inclined to be rather late in coming into bearing.

History. Originated at Orange, California, by C. P. Taft from seed planted in 1900.

QUEEN (Guatemalan)

Fruit. Pyriform, weight one and one-half pounds. Skin thick and woody; deep purple in color. Flesh rich clear yellow, changing to dark green near the skin, and has a rich nutty flavor. Seed very small, completely filling the cavity. Ripens in early summer. This is one of the promising new varieties.

Tree. Vigorous but of somewhat spreading growth; very productive.

History. Introduced by E. E. Knight of Yorba Linda, California, from budwood brought from an elevation of 5,200 feet in Guatemala.

LINDA (Guatemalan)

Fruit. Nearly round, weight about two pounds. Skin rough, thick and woody, deep purple in color. Flesh firm, yellowish in color, with a rich nutty flavor. Seed medium size and tight in cavity. Ripens from October to March in Guatemala.

Tree. Vigorous and hardy, productiveness good.

History. Introduced as budwood from Guatemala in 1914 by E. E. Knight as Knight's No. 39.

PICKING, PACKING AND MARKETING

The ordinary orange clipper is the best for picking Avocados. They should be clipped from the tree at a point just above the swollen part of the stem, usually about one inch from where the steam is attached to the fruit. There has been much discussion with regard to the proper time to pick the fruit, and in the past not a little fruit has been picked and marketed in a green state, a condition to be very much regretted as it has a detrimental effect on the consumption of good fruit. Many more people would now be eating Avocados were it not for the fact that the first one they tried happened to be immature and consequently lacked the rich nutty flavor always found in well-matured fruits.

For home use the Avocado should be left on the tree until it is quite mature. The dark or purple skinned fruit should not be picked until the entire surface, especially around the stem, has changed from green to purple. The green skinned fruit should be left on the tree until the stem has commenced to show a distinct yellow cast and the fruit loses its glossy green color and assumes a dull or yellowish shade.

For market purposes the fruit should be picked at a somewhat earlier stage, but the most suitable time will necessarily have to be ascertained by individual experiments and tests until the California Avocado Association has had sufficient time to compute the maturity standards and dates of ripening of the different varieties. The Association hopes to have this data complete in the near future, at which time the growers will be advised as to what condition the different varieties should be in, to comply with the maturity standard. It is to be hoped that all growers will co-operate with the Association in this work to the end that the practice of marketing either immature or over-ripe fruit will be eliminated.

Up to the present time the local consumption has been sufficient to take care of all the fruit raised in California and little or no attention has been paid to the matter of picking for shipment. In Florida, Avocadoes are packed in tomato crates which are similar to our orange boxes being 12x12x24 inches, divided into two compartments. Coarse excelsior is used between the layers of fruit to prevent bruising. The fruit is not wrapped as this tends to hasten ripening, causing it to reach the market in a soft and unsalable condition.

As the production increases there will no doubt be some uniform method of packing adopted whereby the fruit will present the most attractive appearance and at the same time reach the consumer in the best possible condition. With properly matured fruit put up in attractive packages there is no question but that there will be an ever-increasing demand for this valuable food product that will take care of the production for many years to come.

FOOD VALUE

The Avocado by chemical analysis contains neither acid nor sugar and heads the lists of fruits rich in mineral matter and protein, but its greatest food value lies in its oil content, which, in the better varieties, varies from 17 to 30 per cent of vegetable oil or fat. Most of our fruits analyze 200 to 300 food units per pound expressed in calories, while the Avocado averages 1,000 calories. In fact, it is nature's combination of two types of food—fruit and oil.

The Avocado and the Olive are practically the only two fruits that contain any notable amount of fat or oil. The latter fruit has the disadvantage of requiring processing before it is ready for consumption, and should really rank as a processed fruit. The Avocado stands higher in oil content than the olive. It ranks with milk and eggs and is fully equal to lean meat. It has the medicinal quality of a soothing laxative and is more easily assimilated than either dairy butter or meat.

In Africa the Avocado, in addition to being consumed regularly, is rendered like lard and butter and in this way made to produce a commodity similar to butter and fully as apetizing and nutritious.

ACQUIRING A TASTE FOR THE AVOCADO

THE flesh of the Avocado has a delicate, rich nutty flavor and a smooth buttery texture which is very pleasant and satisfying.

People best acquainted with the Avocado, especially those from the tropics, prefer it just as nature has perfected it, without any seasoning, liking the natural, delicious nutty flavor unchanged by condiments. The flavor strikes the palate at once as different, and the taste for it sometimes needs to be cultivated. Possibly the best way for the novice to do this is to use a little lime or lemon juice and sugar, if preferred, which seems to bring out the delicate flavor and the qualities of the fruit, and also supplies the acid and sugar contents which the Avocado lacks and people are accustomed to in all of our common fruits. After a short time he will invariably find himself thoughtlessly omitting these additions and will commence to appreciate the natural delicate qualities of the fruit. Many people prefer simply the addition of salt, and if the flesh is first slightly scored or slashed with the knife or fork before adding the salt and then allowed to set for a few minutes until the salt has dissolved and mixed with the oil of the fruit, the rich nutty flavor seems to be brought out more prominently.

The fruit as picked from the tree is hard and inedible, and should not be used until it has softened or mellowed so that when pressed it yields to the slight pressure of the finger or leaves a slight indented impression in the skin, showing that the flesh has become mellow like an apple or pear. This usually requires from seven to fourteen days after picking, according to whether the temperature is hot or cold where the fruit is kept. After the proper ripening stage is reached they remain only a few days in a fit condition to eat. Ripening may be hastened by placing the fruit in boxes filled with straw, leaves, or similar material. Some claim that the fruit ripens more evenly when these boxes are kept in a warm place. The Avocado may be served with any course of food from soup to nuts.

AVOCADO RECIPES

Half-shell. Cut the fruit in halves and remove the seed. Serve one half to each person, natural, or with lime or lemon juice, or salt as previously described. The flesh of the fruit is scooped out of the shell with a spoon. As a breakfast dish this is very much appreciated and most easily digested.

Avocado au Natural. Remove the skin and slice the fruit as thin as desired. Serve on a plate garnished with celery hearts or with tomatoes. To be eaten with a fork, with or without salt as preferred.

Avocado Sandwich. One that may be recommended for its healthfulness as well as for its flavor, has a thick layer of well salted crushed avocado filling with very thin slices of peeled lime or lemons.

Hawaiian Sandwich. Remove skin and seed, or scoop out flesh from hard shelled varieties, mash the flesh very fine, season to taste with salt, lime or lemon juice, and spread liberally on a lettuce leaf placed between thin slices of bread. No butter should be spread on the bread as the Avocado is a complete and better ingredient to use. This is a dainty and most delicious way of serving.

On Toast. Remove flesh with a spoon and mash with a fork. Spread thickly on a mall square of hot toast. Add a little salt. This is one of the nicest ways of serving the Avocado.

In Soups. The Avocado is used extensively in the tropics in all kinds of meat soups. Cut in small cubes and add to the soup just before serving. The flavor imparted is exceedingly pleasant.

With Nuts and Olives. Chop nuts and olives, mix with an equal quantity of mashed Avocado. Spread between thin slices of bread and butter, with lettuce. Mix ground walnuts with Avocado pulp to thick paste and spread on thin Graham bread or wafers. Also makes fine addiion to any salad.

Avocado Ice Cream. (1) One gallon cream, one pound sugar, pulp of sixteen medium sized Avocados. Rub Avocados through a seive, add to cream and freeze. (2) Yolks of five eggs, one quart milk, green maraschino cherries. two cups sugar, four medium size Avocados, almond or vanilla extract. Make a boiled custard of milk, eggs and sugar; flavor. When cool add the fruit and freeze. A maraschino cherry on top of each dish is an attraction.

These recipes were selected on account of their simplicity, but the thoughtful housewife can enlarge upon them and find many ways of combining and serving the Avocado. The fruit is used very extensively in salads of all kinds.

A Montezuma tree in Guatemala, producing 3000 fruits per annum averaging 1½ pounds each.

MISCELLANEOUS TROPICAL FRUITS

FEIJOA SELLOWIANA

The Feijoa, (pronounced Fay-zho-a, accenting the middle syllable) sometimes called the Pineapple Guava, is a native of South America and was first introduced into France by Edouard Andre in 1890. From there it was brought to California about 1900, and through the efforts of Dr. Francheschi, of Santa Barbara, calling attention of plant growers to its merits it has attracted considerable popularity.

The plant never attains a height of more than fifteen to eighteen feet. The leaves are similar in form and appearance to those of the olive, the upper surface being a glossy green, and the lower silver gray. This, together with its strikingly handsome flowers makes it a very attractive plant for the garden. The fruit of the improved varieties is from two and a half to four inches long and two to two and a half inches in diameter, of a dull green color overspread with a whitish bloom. The skin is thin, next to which is a light granular flesh surrounding a jelly like pulp containing twenty to thirty minute seeds.

The flavor is pleasing and suggestive of pineapple and strawberry and has an aroma that is delightful and penetrating. The fruit may be eaten fresh as picked from the tree or it may be stewed or made into jam or jelly. It also makes excellent pies.

The Feijoa is hardier than most sub-tropical fruits and will withstand a temperature of 15 degrees above zero with little or no injury. It prefers a dry climate but not one of extremely high temperature. Where planted in the moist tropical regions it has not proven successful. It will stand considerable hardships and is quite drouth-resistant when once established, but reaches perfection

Specimen plant Feijoa choiceana.

only when it is properly irrigated and cultivated. It will thrive on almost any kind of soil excepting where there is a surplus of lime, but it seems to do best on a sandy loam rich in humus. The plants should be set from fifteen to eighteen feet apart and watered liberally while young.

Plants grown from seeds do not come true to type nor are they always self fertile. To insure plants that will produce and be of desirable types we graft all of our Feijoas from the best fruiting sorts.

Choiceana. One of the best large fruiting sorts. Fruits oblong about three inches in length. Is of excellent quality and a good bearer. Ripens in the late Fall.

Superba. Fruit is nearly round and the plant not quite so compact in its growth, otherwise it is similar to the Choiceana.

CHERIMOYA (Anona Cherimolia)

The Cherimoya, sometimes called the Custard Apple, is a native of South America from where it spread northward into Central America and Mexico. It is not strictly a tropical fruit and might be better classed as sub-tropical, as it prefers a cool, relatively dry climate and in its native habitat it only reaches perfection at the higher elevations back from the coast. In Guatemala and Mexico the finest Cherimoyas are to be found at an elevation from 3,000 to 8,000 feet where the climate is mild and no extremes of either heat or cold are experienced. Young plants will be hurt by a temperature of 29 to 30 degrees above zero, but mature trees will stand a temperature as low as 26 or 27 degrees without serious injury.

The tree is erect but has somewhat of a spreading habit and rarely reaches more than twenty-five feet in height. The fruit is usually heart shaped but is sometimes irregular in form. It also varies in weight from a few ounces to as high as five pounds, however, the budded or grafted varieties are more regular in both shape and weight. The surface of the fruit is usually covered with small conical protuberances, is light green in color and has a thin skin making it necessary to handle the ripe fruit very carefully to prevent bruising. The flesh is white and of a melting juicy texture. It has a very delicate sub-acid flavor suggestive of pineapple and banana. When ready to pick, which is from January to April in California, the fruit usually has a yellowish tinge. Under favorable conditions the trees begin to bear the third or fourth year.

Only budded or grafted trees should be planted as seedlings do not always come true and very often are light bearers.

The Cherimoya prefers a rich, loamy soil, but seems to do fairly well on both light and heavy soils, provided climatic conditions are favorable.

Irrigations during the summer months should be applied every two to four weeks according to weather conditions. A thorough cultivation should follow after each irrigation.

It is recommended that the trees be kept pruned to form a low compact head, as this tends to make them longer lived and more precocious.

THE WHITE SAPOTE (Casimiroa edulis)

The White Sapote is a native of Mexico and Central America and is one of the principal cultivated fruits of those regions, being held in very high esteem by the natives. It is sub-tropical in its climatic requirements, and in its native home it thrives best in the highlands at an elevation of from 2,000 to 3,000 feet and is not found where the rainfall is excessive.

It was first introduced into California in about 1810, but until recent years has attracted very little attention. This is no doubt due to the fact that all trees planted were seedlings, which do not come true to type, some bearing small bitter fruit and others being shy bearers, or not bearing any fruit whatever.

The tree is medium sized, erect or spreading in its growth, with compound leaves. The fruit is about the size of an orange and of a yellowish green color. The skin is thin and the yellowish flesh of soft melting texture has a peach-like flavor. Ripens in the Fall and early Winter.

Seedling trees do not come into bearing until seven or eight years old but budded varieties fruit much earlier.

It should be grown on well drained soil, sandy loam being preferable, but will also do well on heavier clay soil, provided the drainage is good.

It is quite drought resistant but will do much better if irrigated about the same as citrus trees. Should not be planted where it is too cold for Avocados.

THE GUAVA

The Guava belongs to the Myrtle family and is said to be a native of tropical America. While it may be used in many ways, its most general use is for jelly making for which purpose it is unexcelled. It is first mentioned in Gonzalo Hernandez de Oviedo's "Natural History of the Indies" written in the year 1526.

STRAWBERRY GUAVA

Fruit. Obovate to round in form, being from one to one and one-half inches in diameter, purplish red in color and medium thick skin. The flesh is pink next to the skin changing to a creamy white in the center and contains a number of small hard seed. When fully mature it has a sweet strawberry flavor. Makes excel-

A handsome and symmetrical White Sapota tree.

The tree rarely attains a height of more than twenty-five feet and for the first few years appears to be more of a shrub than a tree. Most varieties are very prolific and come into bearing at an early age. It is strictly a tropical fruit and should be grown only in sheltered places, although some varieties are more hardy and can be planted safely wherever oranges do well.

It is not particular as to soil as it seems to do equally well on all classes of soil from the lightest sandy loam to the heaviest adobe, however it must have sufficient moisture to produce an abundance of good fruit. Only the hardier varieties are recommended for California planting; the Strawberry and Yellow Strawberry being the hardiest.

lent jellies and can be eaten out of hand when thoroughly ripe. Ripens October and November.

Tree. More of a shrub than a tree, rarely attaining a height of more than twenty to twenty-five feet. Its glossy green leaves make it very attractive as an ornamental plant. Quite hardy and will stand about the same temperature as the orange.

History. It is a native of Brazil but at an early date was carried to China and for many years was considered to be a native of the latter country and was called the Chinese Guava.

Specimen fruit of the Anona Cherimoya or custard apple.

YELLOW STRAWBERRY GUAVA

Fruit. Yellow in color and somewhat larger than the red variety, also has a milder and more delicate flavor. Ripens at the same time.

History. Belongs to the same species and is probably a seed variation.

Tree. Similar in growth and appearance to the red variety and of about the same hardiness.

Massed group of Anona Cherimoya and avocado trees.

TOPICAL INDEX

CITRUS FRUITS

Citrus Fruits:
- Historical 4-8
- Buds From Record Trees 11-12
- Buds Selection 8-11
- Growing Teague Quality Trees 8
- Preparing the Land for Orchard 14-15
- Selecting Good Citrus Land 13-14
- Training the Young Buds 12-13

Methods of Planting:
- Hexagonal or Septuple System 16
- Planting Balled Trees 20
- Planting Open Root Trees 20
- Quincunx System 16
- Selecting Good Trees 18
- Square System 15
- Triangular or Alternate System 16

Care of the Orchard:
- Orchard Management 20-22
- Fertilization 22-24
- Pruning the Orange 24
- Pruning the Lemon 24-25
- Handling the Crop 36-40

Standard Varieties of Oranges
- Homosassa 28
- Joppa 28
- Malta Blood 29
- Mediterranean Sweet 28
- Navelencia 28
- Paper Rind St. Michael 28
- Ruby Blood 29
- Thomson Improved Navel 25
- Valencia Late 25
- Washington Navel 25

Standard Varieties of Lemons:
- Eureka 32
- Lisbon 33
- Villa Franca 33

Standard Varieties Kid Glove Oranges:
- Dancy Tangerine 30
- King Mandarin 30
- Satsuma (Oonshiu) 31
- Willow Leaved Mandarin 31

Standard Limes:
- Mexican Lime 34
- Tahiti Lime 34

Standard Pomelos:
- Duncan Pomelo 35
- Foster Pomelo 35
- Marsh Seedless Pomelo 34
- Triumph Pomelo 34

Kumquats:
- Nagami 31

New and Rare Varieties of Oranges:
- Bitter Seville 30
- Golden Buckeye Navel 29
- Golden Nugget Navel 29
- Lue Gim Gong 29
- Sweet Seville 30
- Vanilla Orange 30

New and Rare Varieties of Lemons:
- Cedrola 33
- Dwarf Lemon 33
- Ponderosa Lemon 33
- Sweet Lemon 33

New Varieties Kid Glove Oranges:
- Algerian Mandarin 32
- Algerian Tangerine 32

New and Rare Varieties of Limes:
- Rangpur Lime (Red Lime) 34
- Sweet Lime 34
- Thornless Lime 34

Ornamental Varieties of Oranges:
- Bouquet des Fleurs 30
- Golden Variegated 30
- Variegated Navel 30

Ornamental Lemons:
- Variegated Lemon 33

Odd Citrus Varieties:
- Bun Tan 35
- Citrange 35
- Citron of Commerce 35
- Sampson Tangelo 35

TROPICAL FRUITS

- Avocados (Historical) 43
- Acquiring a Taste for the Avocado 55
- Climate and Soil 48
- Cultural Directions 50
- Distance to Plant 48
- Early Introduction in California 43-46
- Fertilization 50
- Food Value 55
- Growing and Transplanting Trees 46-47
- Picking, Packing and Marketing 54
- Planting 48
- Planting Season 48
- Pruning 51
- Top Working Avocado Trees 51-52
- Recipes for Preparing Avocados 55

Recommended Varieties:
- Dickenson 53
- Fuerte 53
- Puebla 53
- Sharpless 53
- Spinks 53

Varieties of More or Less Commercial Importance:
- Blakeman 54
- Linda 54
- Lyon 54
- Queen 54
- Taft 54

Cherimoya (Anona Cherimolia) 57

Feijoa Sellowiana 56
- Choiceana Variety 57
- Superba Variety 57

The Guava 58
- Strawberry Variety 58
- Yellow Strawberry Variety 59

The White Sapote (Casimiroa edulis) 57

Made in the USA
Coppell, TX
16 June 2020